MILWAUKEE BRAVES

MILWAUKEE

Braves

HEROES AND HEARTBREAK

William Povletich

WISCONSIN HISTORICAL SOCIETY PRESS

Published by the Wisconsin Historical Society Press
Publishers since 1855

© 2009 by the State Historical Society of Wisconsin

Publication of this book was made possible in part by a grant from the D.C. Everest fellowship fund.

wisconsin**history**.org

Photographs identified with WHi or WHS are from the Society's collections; address requests to reproduce these photos to the Visual Materials Archivist at Wisconsin Historical Society, 816 State Street, Madison, WI 53706.

Frontmatter photo credits:
page ii: Johnny Logan (Robert Koehler Collection); page iii: Henry Aaron (author's collection); page v left: County Stadium scoreboard welcomes the Braves, 1953. (Robert Koehler Collection); page v right: Warren Spahn and Joe Adcock (Robert Koehler Collection); page vi: Eddie Mathews (Bob Buege); page viii: (clockwise from bottom left) Dennis Overby, Dave Fracaro, John Braun, Clair Hickman, Bob Botz, and Bob Uecker, 1961 (Robert Koehler Collection)

Printed in the United States of America
Designed by Percolator, Minneapolis

13 12   2 3 4 5

Library of Congress Cataloging-in-Publication Data
Povletich, William.
    Milwaukee Braves : heroes and heartbreak / William Povletich.
        p. cm.
    Includes bibliographical references and index.
    ISBN 978-0-87020-423-4 (pbk. : alk. paper) 1. Milwaukee Braves (Baseball team)—History. I. Title.
    GV875.M5.P68 2009
    796.357'64077595—dc22

                                                2008043259

This book is dedicated to all of the Milwaukee Braves players,
staff, boosters, and fans who participated in one of the most
amazing chapters of civic pride in American history.

CONTENTS

FOREWORD

"The Miracle of Milwaukee" far exceeded anything I could have imagined while growing up in Southern California. When the Braves franchise moved to Milwaukee in 1953, they were hoping to draw a few more people and make a little more money than they had in Boston. Little did we players realize how tremendous Milwaukee would be as a baseball town, from the first moment we stepped off the train and were greeted by thousands of fans. Many of the Braves were young, like Eddie Mathews and Billy Bruton. Others, like myself and Bob Buhl, had just gotten out of the service. And a handful of veterans, like Warren Spahn and Andy Pafko, were reinvigorated by the community support.

The reception we received from Milwaukee went far beyond the gifts of loaned cars from Wally Rank, milk from Golden Guernsey, meat from Kroeger, and drycleaning from Spic 'n' Span. It was the people who made us all feel very special.

Braves catcher Del Crandall with manager Charlie Grimm (ROBERT KOEHLER COLLECTION)

Regardless of how many World Series titles or attendance records have been broken by a franchise before or since, that relationship between a community and a team will never be duplicated. *Milwaukee Braves: Heroes and Heartbreak* immediately took me back to all those wonderful years of my life. When you read this book, you'll relive the great times in Milwaukee when baseball was the only game in town and people came out in droves to watch us play.

On the field, our manager, Charlie Grimm, was the perfect fit for the Braves during those first few years in Milwaukee. He really knew how to mold us into winners by keeping the clubhouse light and not being very demanding. Us hardnosed players didn't need daily pep talks, so he just let us go out and perform. Although Charlie was not around to lead us into the World Series, we were all tremendously grateful for the opportunities he provided us to grow into Major Leaguers. In 1956, Fred Haney took the reigns from Charlie and was just what we needed. He demanded a lot from us as maturing ballplayers and guided us to a World Series victory in 1957. He knew how to polish us into champions.

Milwaukee Braves: Heroes and Heartbreak will take you on a journey through those glory years—as well as when things started to fall apart. It was obvious to all of us in the clubhouse that something wasn't quite right with Milwaukee baseball after we won the 1957 World Series. But even with the front office's recalibrated approach towards replenishing the aging roster, the beer ban at County Stadium, and the arrival of new ownership, none of us could've predicted the Milwaukee Braves' eventual fate. I remember when I had been traded and came back as a member of the Giants and Pirates, it was obvious the Braves were in a lame-duck situation while rumors swirled about their eventual departure for Atlanta in 1966. As someone who truly cherished his years as a resident of Brookfield, Wisconsin, during my playing days, it broke my heart to witness the final days of the Braves in Milwaukee.

You don't have to be a Milwaukee Braves fan to appreciate *Milwaukee Braves: Heroes and Heartbreak*. Anybody who enjoys baseball, has an appreciation for the cultural significance of professional sports, or calls Wisconsin home will enjoy reading how the Braves became the team that made Milwaukee famous.

—Del Crandall
 Milwaukee Braves catcher from 1953 to 1963
 Team captain
 Eight-time All-Star
 Four-time Gold Glove winner

PROLOGUE

It was an event fifty years in the making. On August 30, 2007, fourteen members of the Milwaukee Braves' 1957 World Series championship team gathered to celebrate the golden anniversary of their historic achievement. Henry Aaron, Red Schoendienst, Del Crandall, Johnny Logan, Wes Covington, and other players shared their memories of winning baseball's world championship for the most devoted fans in baseball. The once-in-a-lifetime celebration offered a glimpse into a clubhouse filled with compelling characters, from future Hall of Famers Warren Spahn and Eddie Mathews to '57 season phenom Bob Hazle and World Series hero Lou Burdette. "I could visualize the old timers telling their young kids that the Milwaukee Braves were their idols," Johnny Logan later gushed.

The daylong celebration began with a dedication outside Milwaukee's Miller Park. Staged in front of a nine-ton monument honoring the 168 players, five managers, and twenty coaches who had worn Milwaukee Braves uniforms, toastmaster Bob Barry announced each player's arrival. Felix Mantilla, John DeMerit, Ray Crone, and Gene Conley greeted the crowd of five hundred dedicated fans with the same charm and charisma that endeared them to Milwaukeeans five decades earlier. It was as if

Toastmaster Bob Barry stands in front of the Milwaukee Braves monument to honor the 1957 World Series team on August 30, 2007. (COURTESY OF RICK SCHABOWSKI)

these ambassadors of Braves baseball never stopped sharing the game they loved with the community that loved them back. "It's good to meet the people who were fans," pitcher Gene Conley said later. "And signing autographs again is fun, you know. It made you feel like you were in the big leagues again!"

As players including Wes Covington, Taylor Phillips, Chuck Tanner, and Carl Willey graciously posed for photos, fans clapped and cheered in an outpouring of affection. It was

Milwaukee Braves
shortstop Johnny Logan
(COURTESY OF RICK
SCHABOWSKI)

a true testament to the team's prominence in the city, an influence that reached its peak when Eddie Mathews stepped on third base to defeat the New York Yankees in Game Seven of the 1957 World Series. Boasting a lineup stocked with future Hall of Famers and All-Stars, the team was immediately embraced by a community yearning for a "big-league" identity. In turn, the Braves captured the hearts and imaginations of millions of fans across the country. "Those fans were tremendous, and we rewarded the fans with some great ball clubs," outfielder Andy Pafko fondly remembered.

By demonstrating how successful a team could be following franchise relocation, the Milwaukee Braves became the darlings of baseball, with record-breaking attendance numbers, spirited booster clubs, and enthusiastic fans arriving from all corners of the Upper Midwest. "Anybody who played baseball in the 1950s and 1960s didn't know what Major League Baseball was all about unless they played in Milwaukee, Wisconsin," legendary pitcher Warren Spahn proclaimed during a 2001 Milwaukee Braves Historical Association banquet in his honor.

But following its 1957 world championship, the team's relationship with its hometown began to sour. After the 1965 season, the Braves abandoned Milwaukee for Atlanta in one of the ugliest divorces between a franchise and a city in professional sports history. But with time the wounds healed, scars faded, and scorned feelings dissipated. Fifty years later, the nostalgia surrounding the Braves legacy

The fourteen members of the 1957 Milwaukee Braves in attendance at the 2007 anniversary event: (from left to right) Hawk Taylor, Red Schoendienst, Johnny Logan, Ray Crone, Chuck Tanner, Taylor Phillips, Felix Mantilla, Wes Covington, Henry Aaron, Del Crandall, Gene Conley, Carl Willey, and John DeMerit (Andy Pafko not pictured) (COURTESY OF RICK SCHABOWSKI)

Milwaukee Braves catcher Del Crandall and outfielder Andy Pafko (COURTESY OF RICK SCHABOWSKI)

> "Anybody who played baseball in the 1950s and 1960s didn't know what Major League Baseball was all about unless they played in Milwaukee, Wisconsin."
>
> —WARREN SPAHN

LEFT: Milwaukee Braves infielder Felix Mantilla (COURTESY OF RICK SCHABOWSKI)

RIGHT: Milwaukee Braves outfielder Henry Aaron (COURTESY OF RICK SCHABOWSKI)

endured. "Today, all I hear is, those old Braves were really great. And these are people from Philadelphia, New York, Detroit, and all over the country," Gene Conley recounted at the anniversary event. "So I think it meant a lot to the whole country."

Although few physical reminders remained after the Braves left Milwaukee, fans soon realized how lucky Wisconsin had been to host some of baseball's greatest talents at County Stadium. And when the stadium was scheduled for demolition in 1999 to make way for Miller Park, former Braves All-Star shortstop Johnny Logan founded the Milwaukee Braves Historical Association in hopes of preserving the team's legacy. "The idea of the association was to have banquets inviting back prominent ballplayers from the Braves team," explained Bob Buege, author of *Milwaukee Braves: A Baseball Eulogy*. "The initial one was to honor Warren Spahn. And in subsequent banquets they honored people like Lou Burdette, Hank Aaron, Del Crandall, and so on."

After its first banquets proved successful as fund-raisers, the Milwaukee Braves Historical Association commissioned the erection of a monument outside Miller Park to immortalize those who sported Milwaukee Braves flannels. Although the Braves' tenure in Milwaukee was brief, the team's influence on the culture of the Upper Midwest and on the overall economic structure of professional sports reached far beyond the baseball diamond. Following his franchise's relocation from Boston to Milwaukee in 1953, Braves owner Lou Perini became the symbol of baseball's new world order. His team's immediate financial success in Milwaukee prompted baseball to redefine itself as a big business and ushered in an era of franchises forgoing civic loyalty and migrating west in search of profits. The nine-ton marble monument at Miller Park does more than celebrate the legacy of the only Major League Baseball franchise in Wisconsin to win a world championship; it represents the inexorable

influence the team that made Milwaukee famous had on the sport of baseball.

Following the dedication at the monument, more than three hundred guests and baseball dignitaries packed Potawatomi Casino's Northern Lights Theater for the celebration's marquee event: a banquet honoring the 1957 world champions. Reminiscing about good times and old friends long departed, each of the fourteen players in attendance took to the podium and reflected on what made the 1957 season meaningful for them. The night reminded everyone in attendance of how magical that year was, for Milwaukee and for the world of baseball. It was obvious the celebration meant as much to the players as it did to the fans. As Felix Mantilla said, "The banquet brought back memories of fifty years ago. It is something that I'll always remember, always remember."

The banquet symbolized how those heroes from that magical 1957 world championship season continue to endure despite the heartbreak of the franchise's controversial relocation to Atlanta following the 1965 season. "So when we talk about the Braves today and their place in history, why people remember them as long as they do, it's because this team was unique," Buege explained. "And the memories are just so strong that it's hard for this community to let go of that team."

The Milwaukee Braves monument at Miller Park (AUTHOR'S COLLECTION)

MILWAUKEE BRAVES

THE *Arrival* 1953

Lou Perini was no dreamy-eyed idealist, and the facts in front of him didn't lie. His Braves baseball team was taking a financial bath in Boston. Relying primarily on gate receipts before the days of lucrative radio or television income, Perini and the Braves were projected to lose approximately $1 million a year based on their current business model. The Braves' owner hadn't become a successful building contractor by accepting mediocrity, and he definitely wasn't going to allow his franchise to fold before his very eyes.

Just weeks following the 1952 season, Perini arranged a top-secret staff meeting with his inner circle. On a gloomy October day, Braves general manager John Quinn, business manager Joe Cairnes, and administrative assistant Chuck Patterson met Perini at his construction company's offices in Framingham, Massachusetts, twenty miles outside of Boston. Perini feared that word of what he was about to disclose would leak out if he held the meeting at the Braves' Boston offices.

Perini outlined the bleak forecast for the Braves ball club in Boston. From 1948 to 1952 the franchise had suffered a devastating 80 percent drop in attendance. The team had lost more than $1 million from 1950 to 1952. Unable to compete with the Boston Red Sox for fan loyalty or revenue, the 1952 Braves had drawn a paltry 281,278 fans—an average of 3,677 a game—and finished seventh in the eight-team National League with a 64–89 record. Although the Boston Braves had been a charter member of baseball's National League in 1876, the franchise's sporadic success had yielded only three seasons in which attendance topped one million.

"He told us the Braves couldn't be competitive in Boston, based on market surveys, and that the future there was bleak," recalled Patterson. "Then he told us not to say a word to anyone, not even our wives." Perini told his executives that no major

The Braves' relocation to Milwaukee was headline news on March 18, 1953. (ROBERT KOEHLER COLLECTION)

league team had relocated in half a century and that leaving Boston would take an audacious act. It was a sound business move, but still it was the hardest decision of his life. Perini told those gathered at the meeting that there was only one solution: "We're moving to Milwaukee."

The winter of 1952 was a time of unrest in America. The Korean War continued to rage half a world away. The civil rights movement was slowly advancing on the American consciousness. The Cold War intensified. In Washington, D.C., Wisconsin's own senator Joseph McCarthy was only months away from his Communist witch hunts on Capitol Hill.

Back in Wisconsin, the state's only metropolis had become a prosperous city in the wake of World War II. With strong industrial companies like Allen-Bradley, A.O. Smith, Allis-Chalmers, and several breweries, Milwaukee's residents were proud blue-collar laborers. Although television was evolving into the newest source of family entertainment, the community continued to support its successful minor-league baseball franchise, the Milwaukee Brewers. Since their arrival in 1902, the Brewers had established a winning tradition as the second-most-successful team in the minor-league American Association's history by consistently contending for the pennant. The team's loyal fans took great pride in cheering for their heroes at the sun-soaked wooden stands of Borchert Field on the city's north side. Still, despite being one of the Boston Braves' most successful farm clubs, Milwaukee was searching for a national identity that would garner the city the respect of metropolises like New York, Chicago, and Philadelphia.

The common factor associated with every "major" American city after World War II was Major League Baseball. Milwaukee had been without a big-league franchise since 1901, when the American League's fledgling Brewers shuffled off to St. Louis to become the Browns after one lackluster season. Although Milwaukee hosted the Green Bay Packers for a portion of their home schedule each season, professional football wasn't considered a marquee sport like America's Pastime was. Aspiring to lure the major leagues to Wisconsin with facilities capable of hosting a franchise, Milwaukee's civic leaders proactively pushed through plans in 1950 to build a modern baseball park.

Despite having the formal approval to build its publicly funded ballpark, Milwaukee endured several delays during County Stadium's construction. When Congress passed a measure to lease twenty-two acres of federally owned land to the county for one dollar a year, the county had to arrange to buy another ninety-eight acres. Once the city deeded additional land to the county, ground was broken at the Story Quarry site in Milwaukee's Menomonee River Valley on October 19, 1950. But one week later construction was temporarily halted by the National Production Authority, which considered the required steel and other building materials vital for the Korean War

> "He told us not to say a word to anyone, not even our wives."
> —CHUCK PATTERSON

effort. A labor union strike also temporarily halted work. Despite delays, the stadium slowly grew from a onetime garbage dump into a cement-and-steel-girder beacon that would guide a major-league franchise to Milwaukee.

Constructing County Stadium without a guaranteed major-league suitor required a leap of faith that made many in the community nervous. There were no guarantees that Milwaukee's state-of-the-art stadium would land a franchise, but without it, the city would never have a chance of obtaining a big-league team.

The minor-league Milwaukee Brewers called Borchert Field home for fifty-one seasons from 1902 through 1952. (ALL-AMERICAN SPORTS, LLC)

By the spring of 1953 the situation looked bleak. Major League Baseball had no immediate plans for expansion, and its last franchise shift had been in 1903, when Baltimore relocated to New York and eventually became the Yankees. With a ballpark financed entirely by public funds at a cost of nearly $6 million, and no prospective big-league tenants publicly interested in Milwaukee, the city was preparing to cut its losses and move the minor-league Brewers out of Borchert Field and into County Stadium for the start of the '53 season.

Back in Boston, the Braves departed for spring training in the sleepy Florida town of Bradenton. With every public intention of returning to Boston by Opening Day, Perini covertly planned his next move. But the Braves weren't the only club pondering a move to Milwaukee.

Also interested in Milwaukee and its new stadium was Bill Veeck, the eccentric owner of the American League's perennial losers, the St. Louis Browns. An owner of the minor-league Milwaukee Brewers from 1941 to 1945, during which the team won three pennants, Veeck was popular among Milwaukee's city elders. Like the Braves in Boston, Veeck's Browns franchise was strapped for cash and unable to compete with St. Louis's more popular team, the Cardinals. After receiving support from boosters Clifford Randall of the Greater Milwaukee Committee and Alvin Monroe of the Milwaukee Association of Commerce Convention Bureau, during the first few months of 1953 Veeck made public his intentions to relocate the Browns to Milwaukee.

Eccentric St. Louis Browns owner Bill Veeck (right) was popular among Milwaukee's civic boosters. (NATIONAL BASEBALL HALL OF FAME LIBRARY)

FACING PAGE: Milwaukee County Stadium was the first major-league ballpark financed entirely by public funds. (ROBERT KOEHLER COLLECTION)

As the current owner of the minor-league Milwaukee franchise, Perini had exclusive territorial rights to the city under baseball's monopolistic operating agreement. To permit the struggling St. Louis Browns franchise to transfer, Veeck and the city needed Perini to give up his territorial rights to Milwaukee. Offering to compensate the Braves $500,000 to move the Brewers, Veeck continued his public pressure and forced Perini's hand. On March 3, 1953, Perini's Braves invoked territorial privilege and blocked the Browns' attempted shift to Milwaukee. Claiming that the $500,000 offer to move the Brewers wasn't sufficient, Perini proposed to fellow owners a ban on *any* major-league franchise moving to a minor-league city before December 1, 1953.

Perini's actions frustrated Milwaukeeans, who chastised him in the press for blocking their aspirations and demanded that their city be allowed to join the major leagues. "You don't know all the letters, telegrams, and telephone calls I've been getting on this thing," Perini complained to fellow owners.

Even though Perini invoked territorial rights, the American League owners could still approve the Browns' move, essentially vanquishing the Braves' owner. As Veeck continued to threaten moving his Browns to Milwaukee, Perini was quickly

losing ground in the court of public opinion. Without the support of National League president Warren Giles, who felt a franchise shift required at least a year for a smooth transition, Perini began privately negotiating with Milwaukee's civic officials. But by Friday, March 13, Perini's private intentions went public when *The Sporting News* claimed that the Braves were planning to relocate to Milwaukee and the Browns to Baltimore before the start of the season. "A Milwaukee baseball reporter named Sam Levy asked Perini if it was true," Eddie Mathews recalled. "His answer was, 'I can't confirm it, and I can't unconfirm it.' When he didn't deny it, everybody knew it was true."

Many in Boston believed that native son Perini considered his Braves a sacred trust, and nobody thought he'd go through with moving the team out of his hometown. The press perceived his evasiveness as a stalling tactic and thought he would eventually tell Milwaukee no, *after* the Browns relocated to Baltimore. But the next day during a press conference, Perini took everybody by surprise and announced his intention to ask the National League owners' permission to move the Braves from Boston to Milwaukee—effective immediately.

Critics considered the announcement a desperation move by a floundering franchise. Perini had to tread carefully, still needing approval from the National League's seven other owners and skeptical league president Warren Giles. For such a drastic experiment, receiving a unanimous vote of approval would be difficult on short notice. Just three days after Perini made his intentions public, the American League rejected Veeck's attempt to move the Browns. Citing broadcast and concession contracts in place for the coming season, baseball commissioner Ford Frick told the press, "The timing is bad right now." With Veeck's desperate attempt to relocate the Browns vanquished by American League owners, some observers thought the precedent was set and National League owners would unanimously refuse Perini's request to move.

Boston Braves vice president Joe Cairnes (center) met with Milwaukee boosters Frederick Miller, president of Miller Brewing Company (left), and Walter Bender, president of the Milwaukee Park Commission (right), to discuss the possibility of a move to County Stadium. (DAVID KLUG COLLECTION)

On the morning of March 18, 1953, the Vinoy Park Hotel in St. Petersburg, Florida, was buzzing with anticipation. National League owners had convened behind closed doors to debate the Braves' fate. After nearly three and a half hours, the meeting adjourned. League president Warren Giles emerged to announce that the owners had unanimously approved the Braves' relocation to Milwaukee. Giles explained that the transfer represented an economic opportunity for the entire National League. Since the teams shared gate revenues, they all suffered if one team had marginal attendance. "There was no real opposition," Giles proclaimed to the press.

Braves Sid Gordon, Andy Pafko, and Billy Bruton talked with the Brooklyn Dodgers' Jackie Robinson a few days before the Braves announced their relocation to Milwaukee. (AUTHOR'S COLLECTION)

The decision stunned those who had expected the Braves to suffer the same fate as Bill Veeck's St. Louis Browns. Giles called the "fine standing and prestige of Perini in our league" a deciding factor.

Observers later speculated that American League owners didn't care for Veeck and wanted him out of baseball. His maverick ideas for elimination of the reserve clause, revenue sharing among the teams, and innovative team marketing were unpopular among baseball's other owners, who hoped that if the Browns were denied the chance to relocate and kept suffering in St. Louis, Veeck would eventually abandon the franchise—which he did a year later.

With the landmark announcement about the Braves, Major League Baseball's landscape had been altered for the first time in half a century. As Warren Giles's announcement rang through the Vinoy Park Hotel's hallways, Milwaukee reporters hustled to their typewriters. The front-page headline in the *Milwaukee Sentinel* screamed, "WE'RE THE HOME OF THE BRAVES!"

◆ ◆ ◆

Nobody was more grateful for the opportunity to play in front of the Milwaukee fans than recent Braves acquisition Andy Pafko. In an interview years later, he recalled, "I'll never forget, we're in spring training and we're playing the St. Louis Cardinals in St. Petersburg, Florida. And before the game started, they made a public announcement that the Boston Braves had become the Milwaukee Braves. And all the guys were thrilled, because Boston was strictly a Red Sox town—Ted Williams and all those great players. Of course I was thrilled too, because that's my home state. How lucky can a guy get?"

> **"How lucky can a guy get?"**
> —ANDY PAFKO

For Braves manager Charlie Grimm, the news of the team's relocation came in the form of symbolic new headwear. "On the day the historic story broke," he wrote in his 1968 autobiography, *Jolly Cholly's Story*, "I was knocking balls to the infielders when [Braves general manager] John Quinn walked onto the field with an armful of baseball caps initialed with 'M.' He told us all to put them on." Although the team's switching from "B" to "M" on the caps was the only physical change to the Braves' uniforms, the move to Milwaukee, in the central time zone, created a challenge of a different sort. The Braves switched schedules with the Pittsburgh Pirates to resolve conflicts with their East Coast starting times and night game schedule.

The first official Milwaukee Braves team photo featured a mix of "B" and "M" logos. (COURTESY OF BOB BUEGE)

Milwaukee Sentinel cartoonist Frank Marasco captured the eagerly anticipated marriage of Milwaukee and the Braves. (COURTESY MARQUETTE UNIVERSITY ARCHIVES, FRANK J. MARASCO CARTOON COLLECTION)

Opening Day was less than a month away, and the Braves faced the daunting task of selling tickets in Milwaukee without having had any off-season marketing or advertising. Planning to chain off the upper grandstand to save on maintenance expenses, Perini was optimistic that if the Braves could draw more than one million in attendance, the franchise move would be deemed a success. However, playing in the second-smallest city in the majors, population 725,000, the Braves would have to rely on support from surrounding communities and the rest of Wisconsin, Iowa, Minnesota, and northern Illinois to achieve their optimistic goal. "If five years from now this move has proved successful," Lou Perini pronounced in the Braves' 1953 Yearbook, "and I have contributed something to baseball, I will be very pleased."

With the Braves moving to Milwaukee, the minor-league Brewers franchise was hastily relocated to Toledo, Ohio, in time for the 1953 season. As Opening Day approached, Braves officials had no idea how they'd be received in Milwaukee, especially after displacing the beloved minor-league Brewers. "You can't imagine the complex situation which arose," Braves executive vice president Joseph Cairnes remembered. "When we put our Opening Day tickets on sale, we offered to exchange any tickets which fans had purchased in advance for

Crowded ticket windows at County Stadium were the norm during the 1953 season. (MILWAUKEE JOURNAL SENTINEL)

the Brewers opening game and to give them as nearly as possible the same locations." The Braves' ticket office anticipated a small crowd, but Cairnes said, "It turned out there were plenty of fans in the lines without tickets to exchange who were eager to buy tickets for the Braves opener, more eager than I guessed. They were buying them by the dozens!"

Milwaukee had good reason to be enthusiastic. The Braves were bringing an exciting brand of professional baseball to fans throughout the Upper Midwest—many of whom had never witnessed a major-league game in person. "People were bringing cash, and we didn't know where to stuff it," Roland Hemond, then a young Braves official, recalled.

Fans and local businesses clamored for the opportunity to be part of the big-league atmosphere. "You couldn't go into a store and not see a sign or something about the Braves," Milwaukee Braves historian Bob Buege remembered. Even local post offices proudly stamped outgoing mail "Home of the Braves," proclaiming Milwaukee's new major-league status. Fans could join the Milwaukee Braves Booster Club for twenty-five cents; by season's end the club boasted more than ten thousand members with representation in 262 Wisconsin communities and another two hundred in thirty-six states.

The Braves' appeal crossed all demographic boundaries, from factory workers to the city's rich and famous, and the team's ticket office was inundated with requests from all over Wisconsin. As soon as one pile of requests was opened, sorted, and filled, more arrived, causing the boxes and baskets to constantly overflow. The demand for tickets became so intense that some home stands sold out weeks in advance.

As surprised as everyone was with the Braves' initial ticket sales, the ball club was apprehensive about long-term success. After enduring decades of losing baseball in Boston, the franchise showed no signs of improving on its seventh-place finish in 1952. Team officials knew the novelty of major-league baseball in Milwaukee would quickly wear off if the Braves didn't start winning in their new home. "Despite the electric response, I think there were some reservations," manager Charlie Grimm remembered. "Milwaukee had inherited a sick club."

When spring training concluded back in Bradenton, Florida, the Braves loaded their equipment truck with bats, gloves, uniforms, and a steep baseball tradition from the team's eighty-two years in Boston. Milwaukee was about to become home to the oldest continuously operating pro sports franchise in America. The Boston Braves won professional baseball's first league game in 1871; by the time the Red Sox were established in 1901, the Braves had already won twelve pennants. The "Miracle Braves" of 1914 enjoyed one of the biggest sports upsets in the first half of the twentieth century, rising from last place on the Fourth of July to overtake the New York Giants for the National League pennant, en route to sweeping four straight from the Philadelphia Athletics to win the World Series. Following the 1914 miracle came a three-decade malaise, and the Braves' win-loss record topped .500 only five times through 1945, with the low point in 1935 when the team lost 115 of 154 games. During their decades-long slump, the Braves tried to fill seats by signing stars well past their prime, including Olympian Jim Thorpe and legendary home-run hitter Babe Ruth. The team tried reinventing itself with various nicknames, including the Red Stockings, the Beaneaters, the Doves, the Rustlers, and the Bees. When Lou Perini and associates Guido Rugo and Joseph Maney, known collectively as the Three Little Steam Shovels, took control of the franchise in 1944, they rebuilt the Braves using an approach that had made their respective construction businesses immensely profitable during World War II. Perini soon centralized the ownership group by buying out his two fellow steam shovels and turned the Braves into an all-Perini enterprise, with brother Charley as first vice president and brother Joe as treasurer. The tremendous front office overhaul resulted in the team contending for a pennant soon after. But despite the efforts of the pitching duo of "Spahn, Sain and Pray for Rain," Boston's Cinderella season of 1948 ended with a World Series defeat by the Cleveland Indians. Afterward, the Braves again slumped badly, to fourth-place finishes the following three seasons and a disastrous seventh-place fall in 1952. With the crosstown

Red Sox continually drawing more than one million fans to Fenway Park, few Bostonians seemed to notice as the Braves' equipment truck departed spring training and headed west toward the unproven major-league baseball frontier of Wisconsin. The Boston orphans were still uncertain how they'd be received during their first appearance in Milwaukee.

> **"I don't think any city has ever gone as crazy over a baseball team."**
>
> —EDDIE MATHEWS

Despite chilly weather conditions, more than twelve thousand ecstatic fans greeted the Braves at the train station as they pulled into town on April 8, 1953. The team was escorted from the train platform across a red carpet to open-air cars. Veteran Braves catcher Walker Cooper, who had endured numerous losing seasons in Boston, beamed as he approached his awaiting convertible that day: "This reception is getting better all the time."

Almost immediately the players, coaches, and Braves management were waving to sixty thousand admirers in a parade down Wisconsin Avenue—just part of Mayor Frank Zeidler's proclaimed week of celebration honoring Milwaukee's new status as a major-league city. "All along the route the people were packed three or four deep and screaming and waving like we were heroes or something," third baseman Eddie Mathews remembered. "I don't think any city has ever gone as crazy over a baseball team."

Thousands of exuberant youngsters sporting newly printed Milwaukee Braves T-shirts waved their pennants, pins, and badges as confetti and streamers floated down from the buildings. The Blatz, Schlitz, and Miller bands belted out polkas. "The reaction of the players was something to see," Lou Perini said later. "They were all choked up, their features frozen with surprise. There never had been anything like this in Boston, even after we won the pennant in 1948."

Sitting alongside Perini was brewery magnate and Milwaukee native Frederick Miller. For Miller, a onetime Notre Dame football captain and a sports fanatic, the Braves' arrival in Milwaukee was a dream come true. "It would be hard to overstate how much Fred Miller had meant to the city of Milwaukee," Mathews recalled.

As one of the Braves' biggest boosters in Milwaukee from the beginning, Miller, along with William McGovern of the Wisconsin Telephone Company, helped convince Perini that moving to Milwaukee wouldn't be a mistake. "My ambition is to make Milwaukee a sports center," vowed Miller, "and keep it that way." Miller had even helped negotiate one of baseball's first "sweetheart" stadium leases—allowing the Braves to pay just $1,000 a year to rent County Stadium. "More than anybody else, Fred Miller was responsible for the Braves moving from Boston to Milwaukee," Mathews remarked. "He was the driving force behind the construction of County Stadium. . . . He put the support of his brewery and all their advertising dollars behind the Braves and persuaded Lou Perini to make the shift."

For Braves manager Charlie Grimm, the parade was something of a homecoming. After two very successful stints as the manager of the minor-league Milwaukee

TOP: The parade through downtown Milwaukee introduced nearly sixty thousand frenzied fans to their new team. (ROBERT KOEHLER COLLECTION)

MIDDLE ROW, LEFT: Alongside Lou Perini during many of the welcoming festivities was Milwaukee brewery magnate Frederick Miller. (COURTESY OF BOB BUEGE)

MIDDLE ROW, RIGHT: Braves rookie center fielder Billy Bruton was flanked by fans Dorothy Ihling (left) and Janet Schmidt (right) as they waved to exuberant fans along Wisconsin Avenue. (DAVID KLUG COLLECTION)

BOTTOM: Overwhelmed by the crowds, several Braves players needed nearly an hour to get from the train platform to their cars. (ROBERT KOEHLER COLLECTION)

Brewers from 1941 to 1943 and again from 1949 through part of the 1952 season, Grimm was no stranger to the Borchert Field faithful. He had intended to finish his distinguished career with the Braves' top affiliate farm club after the Brewers won the 1951 American Association crown. Hoping Grimm could recapture the success he enjoyed while managing the Cubs to three National League pennants during the 1930s, Perini had handpicked him as the Braves' field manager in the middle of the 1952 season. Within less than a year, the banjo-strumming skipper was returning to Milwaukee, this time as the manager of the city's major-league franchise. Upon his return Grimm was being feted like a local folk hero, and the Braves manager couldn't help but beam at "the greatest reception any ball club received from any town."

Despite the city's warm welcome, the raw Wisconsin weather froze out County Stadium's attempt at hosting its first game on April 10. The exhibition contest between the Braves and their former crosstown rival Red Sox was called after just two innings due to freezing rain. The inclement weather continued, and the next day's game was canceled before it even started.

With the 1953 regular season upon them, the Braves traveled to Cincinnati for Opening Day. On April 13, more than thirty thousand enthusiastic fans packed Crosley Field only to see their Redlegs (the Cincinnati Reds officially changed their team nickname in 1953 to avoid associations with Communism) handcuffed in a three-hit shutout by the Braves' Max Surkont. In the Braves' 2–0 victory, rookie center fielder Billy Bruton got Milwaukee's first hit, stolen base, and run. Bruton was just as dominating on defense, practically traversing the entire outfield in a single stride. Bruton's leaping catches killed three Redlegs' rallies, and a grateful Surkont bragged to reporters, "In Boston last year, without Bruton, we'd have lost, 8–2."

> **"I threw the first pitch and a tremendous roar went up from the crowd."**
> —WARREN SPAHN

Milwaukee was eager to prove that it was ready to support a major-league baseball team, and the next morning the first of 34,357 fans arrived at 7:30 a.m. for the home opener. As the sellout crowd crammed into the stadium, dignitaries sat alongside regular folks wherever they could find seats. Because construction to seat the ballpark's official capacity of 36,011 had yet to be completed, workers quickly assembled temporary outfield bleachers to accommodate the overflow crowd. One of the most notable makeshift arrangements was the outfield wall: a four-foot-high chain-link fence that would play a big role in deciding the outcome of County Stadium's inaugural game.

The Braves took the field to face the St. Louis Cardinals under gray skies with temperatures in the high forties. When the plate umpire cried out, "Play ball," the Braves' Warren Spahn went to work. The Milwaukee pitching ace took the sign, wound up, kicked, and threw a fastball down the plate to the Cardinals' Solly Hemus. Spahn described it years later: "I'll never forget the first game I pitched in Milwaukee after the Braves moved from Boston. I threw the first pitch and a tremendous roar went up from the crowd."

The County Stadium crowd hung on every one of Spahn's effortless pitches. As his already renowned pitching form coordinated itself into one continuously smooth operation, wasting no motion from windup and kick to step and throw, Spahn kept the Cardinals hitless for the first four innings.

The Braves broke the pitching stalemate in the second inning when Del Crandall hit a slow roller off St. Louis's Gerry Staley that third baseman Ray Jablonski errantly threw toward first. Joe Adcock crossed home plate on the error, scoring County Stadium's first run. Spahn gave up the stadium's second run in the fifth to the Cardinals. Battling back in the eighth, the Braves pulled ahead with a run, but the Cardinals countered in the ninth. With the teams tied at 2, Spahn and Staley carried their mound battle into extra innings.

With one out in the bottom of the tenth, Billy Bruton stepped to the plate and stared down the Cardinals' hurler. The Braves' leadoff man recalled that Staley "threw me a knuckleball, and I liked the looks of it." Bruton's hit soared toward the makeshift right-field seats as the Cardinals' Enos Slaughter tried to catch up with the ball's descending trajectory. At the last second, it seemed the Cardinals' outfielder had made the catch, but as he came down with the ball, his elbow hit the chain-link fence. "The ball slipped off his glove, out of play, to make Warren Spahn the winner and turn thirty-four thousand spectators slightly insane," Charlie Grimm remembered. As he circled the bases, Bruton noticed that the cheering crowd suddenly fell silent. Umpire Lon Warneke had signaled a ground-rule double, believing that a fan had interfered with Slaughter's catch. An angry Grimm charged out of the dugout to protest as

> **"This is just the start of a great year for us, boys."**
> —LOU PERINI

Warren Spahn thought his first offering to the Cardinals' Solly Hemus (7) was a strike. Umpire Jocko Conlan thought it was low and called it a ball. (ROBERT KOEHLER COLLECTION)

Bruton pulled up at third base. Following an animated argument with the umpires, Grimm got the call reversed. Bedlam ensued as Bruton finished circling the bases. The crowd rocked with chants of "Bruton! Bruton! Bruton!" As Bruton crossed home plate, finalizing the Braves' 3–2 victory, his teammates mobbed him.

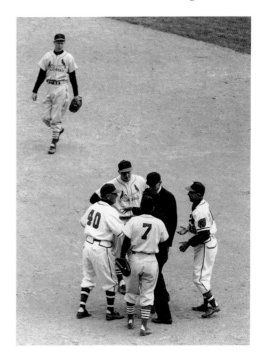

The celebration continued in the Braves' clubhouse as Spahn embraced Bruton in front of reporters. "Keep this up and you'll be greater than Stan Musial," Spahn proclaimed. Pitcher Vern Bickford felt the Braves' center fielder "could run for mayor here tomorrow and win." Even Lou Perini joined in the celebration, predicting, "This is just the start of a great year for us, boys."

RIGHT: Braves manager Charlie Grimm (40) eventually convinced umpire Lon Warneke that Billy Bruton's ground-rule double was indeed a home run. (ROBERT KOEHLER COLLECTION)

Billy Bruton and Warren Spahn were all smiles following the Braves' dramatic 1953 Opening Day victory. (DAVID KLUG COLLECTION)

A youthful energy was spreading throughout the clubhouse, and it was quickly obvious that the losing culture that festered in Boston had not relocated to Milwaukee. Rookie Billy Bruton, second baseman Jack Dittmer, and shortstop Johnny Logan filled the everyday lineup alongside catcher Del Crandall, who had just returned from military service. Third baseman Eddie Mathews was coming off a stellar rookie campaign, while off-season acquisitions Joe Adcock and Wisconsin native Andy Pafko gave the team some fresh veteran leadership at first base and in the outfield, and veteran Sid Gordon returned in left field. Following their Opening Day heroics, *Milwaukee Journal* sports editor Russ Lynch wrote, "A new ball club was born Tuesday afternoon."

Although the Braves lost their next game 10–9 to the Redlegs, Bruton connected for three more hits, giving him a total of eight in his first fourteen major-league at bats. The "Speed Merchant of Wilmington, Delaware" was quickly establishing himself as one of the team's stars. Considered by many to be the fastest man in the game, the Braves' newest phenom was already leading the National League in base hits, triples, and stolen bases, and he had a gaudy .424 batting average by the end of his second week in the majors.

As the Braves' wild first month in Milwaukee wound down, Joe Adcock demonstrated his appreciation for the chance to play every day at first base. Although he hadn't played a game of organized baseball until he attended Louisiana State University on a basketball scholarship, Adcock eventually broke into the majors with the Reds. After three unhappy seasons relegated to their outfield so Cincinnati could keep Ted Kluszewski at first base, Adcock had demanded a trade. Recognizing the slugger's unassuming strength, the Braves acquired Adcock prior to the 1953 season in a complicated four-club transaction. Known as a good glove man, Adcock earned the starting first baseman's job within a couple weeks of spring training. "Joe's a good target out there," Grimm told reporters. "He has a good pair of hands and shifts well. I can't remember him dropping a ball."

It was to everyone's surprise, including his own, when on April 29 Adcock launched a towering 475-foot home run off the New York Giants' Jim Hearn into the tenth row of the Polo Grounds' left-center-field bleachers—making him the first major leaguer to hit a home run to that part of the park since its remodeling in 1923.

During the early years at Milwaukee County Stadium, the red lights of the Johnston Cookie Factory sign flashed from beyond the right-field bleachers. (ROBERT KOEHLER COLLECTION)

"I caught the ball with the good part of the bat," Adcock humbly told reporters. "I knew it was well hit, but not that well hit. I never expected to hit one that far and I don't expect to hit another that far." Having helped the Braves defeat the Giants 3–2, the good-natured Adcock endured plenty of ribbing from his teammates following the front-page publicity he earned for the historic home run. After taking much of the cajoling, he mockingly held up his hand in the clubhouse and said, "Gentlemen, I would like to make a statement. I would like to explain how I could hit a ball that far. You see, when I was with the Reds, I roomed with Kluszewski. Then with this club, I am rooming with Mathews. I guess some of their power sort of rubbed off on me."

Five days later, on May 4, another of Milwaukee's emerging superstars began to shine. Dodgers sluggers had knocked around starting pitcher Johnny Antonelli in the first inning, and the Braves faced a 3–0 deficit. Hoping to stop Brooklyn's slugging onslaught, Charlie Grimm called for right-hander Lou Burdette to finish off the bottom of the first inning. Despite having been relegated to the bullpen during the early days of the 1953 season, Burdette was focused on rebounding from his disappointing '52 campaign. Once Burdette stepped onto the mound, he took command of the game and silenced the Dodgers' bats. Finishing off Brooklyn in the ninth inning by fanning Jackie Robinson with the bases loaded, Burdette recorded his first win in a Milwaukee uniform, as the Braves rallied to beat the Dodgers 9–4.

Having performed his relief duties with workmanlike efficiency, Burdette earned a spot in the Braves starting rotation alongside Spahn and Antonelli. By July 26 he was the top pitcher in baseball, with a dominating 7–0 record. Demonstrating that

LEFT: In 1953 Billy Bruton boasted a National League–best twenty-six stolen bases. (WHI IMAGE ID 49343)

CENTER: Until he arrived at Louisiana State University on a college basketball scholarship, Joe Adcock had never played a game of organized baseball. It was his basketball coach, Red Swanson—who was also the school's baseball coach—who handed Adcock his first glove and turned the Coushatta, Louisiana, native into a first baseman and two-sport star in college. (WHI IMAGE ID 54440)

RIGHT: While often listed as Lew Burdette in news accounts and record books, the pitcher preferred the spelling *Lou* in honor of his idol, legendary New York Yankees first baseman Lou Gehrig. (WHI IMAGE ID 54443)

there was no end to his courage on the mound, Burdette continued to pitch in relief between scheduled starts for the remainder of the season. "Lou had a quality about him that you can't teach," recalled Del Crandall. "He just had supreme confidence in himself and knew he was a good pitcher—and pitched like it."

Burdette's usual mate behind the plate was catcher Crandall, who had just returned from a two-year hitch in the army. Discharged just in time to join the Braves for spring training in late February 1953, he arrived with an enthusiastic personality and a riflelike arm that was both accurate and efficient. Assuming the everyday catching duties from veteran Walker Cooper by Opening Day, Crandall was considered by many to be one of the finest young prospects in the game. "He is big and strong, hustles every minute he's on the field and handles pitchers very well," Grimm told reporters.

With thirteen of the sixteen major-league clubs scouting Crandall during his spectacular career at southern California's Fullerton Union High School, the young catcher quickly proved his reddish blond head was useful for something besides hanging a mask. After studying the rosters of the organizations pursuing him and carefully considering all offers, he had decided to sign with the Braves because he sensed they'd need backstop assistance the soonest.

Although known for his handling of pitchers, Crandall won over Milwaukee fans with his hustle and willingness to throw to any base to nip a runner. But being a fan favorite didn't help him with the opposing players who gave Crandall an unmerciful razzing from the bench. "I back up first base and they yell: 'Get behind the plate, Crandall.' And when I back up third I get the same treatment. When I make a bad throw I get it again. But I am going to keep right on doing it," Crandall told reporters. "You won't get anybody out holding on to the thing."

As the season progressed, skipper Charlie Grimm watched his infield improve daily. Joe Adcock's solid glove provided the Braves a beacon of defense at first. Eddie Mathews's 6'1" physique and powerful wrists had already established him as one of the game's brightest young slugging stars, and the third baseman's fielding continued to improve at the hot corner. "You've heard of the Gold Glove Award," Mathews said. "I got the Golden Chest Award. Knock 'em down, throw 'em out."

The keystone combination of Johnny Logan at shortstop and Jack Dittmer at second base paired two of the Braves' most popular players. The County Stadium fans who worked in factories or brewed beer for a living immediately identified with their blue-collar approach to the game. The son of a shoe factory worker, Logan fielded everything he could get his glove on, quickly earning the respect of his manager. "I'm proud to claim Johnny Logan as one of my boys," Grimm wrote years later. "A great competitor who had to fight his way to the big leagues and keep hustling to stay after he got there."

Shortstop Johnny Logan (left) and second baseman Jack Dittmer (right) played for both the minor-league Brewers and the major-league Braves in Milwaukee. Their familiarity with one another helped rank the Braves second in executed double plays during the 1953 season. (WHI IMAGE ID 49359)

Second baseman Jack Dittmer's experiences as an All–Big Ten football star at the University of Iowa made him a tough customer for opposing base runners trying to spoil his relays to first base. "He can make the play and he's strong and quick. He and Logan know each other from the minors and that always helps," Grimm admitted to reporters.

Much of the credit surrounding the Braves' newfound success belonged to the franchise's maturing farm system. Seventeen players on the Braves' 1953 roster had risen through the team's minor-league ranks. Responsible for executing much of the team's roster strategizing was general manager John Quinn. Growing up in one of baseball's most celebrated multigenerational families, John began working under the tutelage of his father, Robert, in 1936, succeeding him as the Braves' general manager in 1945. The younger Quinn oversaw a front-office staff that included John Mullen, the director of the Braves' vast farm system. As one of the youngest men in baseball, Mullen maintained the team's Waycross, Georgia, minor-league training camp, appraised talent, and assigned players throughout the team's ten farm clubs. With four of the Braves' minor-league affiliates winning their respective league pennants and an equal number winning their league playoffs in 1952, the parent club was optimistic the team would continue building on its minor-league teams' success.

Several veterans who had struggled in Boston were turning their careers around in Milwaukee. Few were as successful or as popular in the team's first season in

Milwaukee as right-hander Max Surkont. During the first two months of 1953, the burly fastballer transformed himself from a mediocre pitcher into a strikeout machine, making him an immediate hit in Milwaukee, especially with fans who shared his Polish ancestry. He won nine of his first ten decisions that season, but it was his performance on the damp evening of May 25 at County Stadium that was most memorable.

Despite a forecast of thunderstorms, 24,445 fans showed up to watch Surkont pitch the second game of a doubleheader against the Redlegs. After winning the first game, the Braves jumped on Cincinnati for six runs in the first inning of the second, allowing Surkont, who had above-average control and a good but not overpowering fastball, to concentrate on throwing strikes. The thirty-year-old struck out the last man to face him in the second and then got the side out on strikes in the third and fourth innings. That gave him seven consecutive strikeouts, tying the modern major-league record.

Rain began falling in the fourth inning, putting the game—and Surkont's record—in jeopardy, because four and a half innings must be played for a game to count in the record books. "In order to slow things down, every batter that the Redlegs sent to the plate was taking," Eddie Mathews recalled. "They were under orders not to swing until they had two strikes on them."

Braves general manager John Quinn was well respected throughout baseball as a skillful evaluator of talent and negotiator of ballplayer contracts. (COURTESY MARQUETTE UNIVERSITY ARCHIVES, FRANK J. MARASCO CARTOON COLLECTION)

With Surkont at bat in the bottom of the fourth, the umpires called time and the grounds crew covered the field with the tarp. Following a thirty-three-minute delay, the game resumed in light rain.

The Braves were retired in the bottom of the fourth without incident. Then Surkont struck out Andy Seminick to open the fifth. That made it eight in a row, a modern record—if the top of the fifth inning could be finished. Immediately after Seminick struck out, the umpires again suspended play as the rain intensified. Braves manager Charlie Grimm complained, and the umpires agreed to continue. Surkont retired the next two batters, making the game and his record official. After another forty-minute rain delay, the game was finally completed as Surkont went the distance, striking out 13 in the 10–3 victory and raising his record to 6–0. When the locker room full of reporters asked Surkont to identify the pitch that fanned Seminick, Surkont replied, "It was the spitter." Although nobody knows for sure if he was kidding, there was plenty of moisture available that evening as Max Surkont inscribed his name in the record books.

Entering June, the Braves continued to prove they were no early-season fluke. Just months after they stopped the Dodgers' eight-game winning streak, they beat Brooklyn again on June 2 to halt their ten-game winning streak at Ebbets Field. Back in Wisconsin, the Braves' ascension in the National League standings fueled their popularity throughout Milwaukee and beyond. Signs on the doors of small businesses across the state read, "Gone to See the Braves. Be Back in Two Days." In Kewaunee County, an Algoma hamburger stand grilled up Bravesburgers. Twenty miles north of Milwaukee, the village of Cedarburg, with a population of 2,500, bought 3,000 tickets and filled every seat. As the Braves' popularity continued to spread across the Upper Midwest, fans from more than a dozen states made trips to watch them in person. Iowans arrived by train. Michigan fans ferried across Lake Michigan with their cars. Parties from the Twin Cities drove down in caravans; Illinois fans traveled in buses. People arrived from all over, causing unforeseen demands on the County Stadium parking lots. "The Braves thus became the first of the 'area' Major League clubs," Charlie Grimm explained in *Jolly Cholly's Story*. "Before this switch, all teams were strictly identified with the city they represented."

Max Surkont was part of a Braves pitching staff that in 1953 led the National League with a 3.30 earned run average. (DAVID KLUG COLLECTION)

Able to hold ten thousand cars comfortably, County Stadium parking lots were stretched beyond their limit. There were so many buses arriving on a daily basis that the stadium's original forty bus spaces were doubled to eighty, but the overflow continued. The parking problem escalated into a full-blown crisis during a Chicago Cubs night game in July when 150 buses created the king of all traffic jams. As buses lined up to get to the stadium, traffic backed up nearly a mile and a half into the city streets.

Buses and cars weren't the only way to travel to the ballpark. The Milwaukee Road train system was inundated with so many ticket requests that by midseason it built a passenger platform where its rails passed County Stadium.

It had become almost as hard to get to the stadium as it was to secure a seat for the game. With admissions ranging from $3.60 for a mezzanine box seat to 75 cents for a view from the bleachers, going to a Braves game was the biggest bargain in town.

As the Braves continued winning, the nation took notice of the energy emanating from the County Stadium crowds. One fan felt the arrival of the Braves was "the greatest thing that has happened to Milwaukee since beer." The euphoria intensified as singing trios and small two- or three-piece bands crashed cymbals, blared accordions, and strummed banjos to help prompt their home-team rallies, and fans using bells, horns, and sirens assisted in the cheering. "Right from the beginning, the fans began to scream at every good play. You could almost see the players respond to it, and pretty soon they were making fantastic plays almost every day," Braves radio announcer Earl Gillespie gushed.

Helping to fuel the fans' growing interest in the Braves, the city's afternoon newspaper, the *Milwaukee Journal*, began running a daily attendance thermometer

The Braves Boosters quickly grew into one of the largest fan clubs in baseball. (DAVID KLUG COLLECTION)

comparing the Braves' 1953 attendance draw against the previous season in Boston. By the thirteenth game of the season on May 20, the Braves and County Stadium had surpassed the team's entire 1952 home attendance of 281,278. With that number conquered so early in the season, the *Journal* replaced the 1952 draw thermometer with the attendance of the Braves' National League pennant–winning season of 1948: 1.45 million.

Amid all the wins and the fanfair, it didn't take long for the players to forget Boston, including Max Surkont. The Pawtucket, Rhode Island, native told a reporter, "Boston has always meant home for me, but for baseball it can't compare with Milwaukee. Every day is Christmas for us. Milwaukee is out of this world."

The fans' fervor didn't stop when the games were over. The players were constantly inundated with autograph requests. "There are those enthusiastic youngsters you find in every baseball community. They usually write fan mail in printed letters so large they hardly get a dozen words on a page," Andy Pafko told a reporter. "About an hour after one home game, I arrived at my car to find an old lady, supported by a cane and the arm of a friend, patiently waiting for my autograph. Her long wait told me how strongly she felt about the Braves."

Players once shunned in Boston now rarely picked up restaurant checks and were showered with gifts of cookies, cigars, suits, and televisions. "Businesses gave us cases of Miller, bought us gas and did our dry cleaning. They treated us like kings," Jack Dittmer recalled. "The people adored us, and we couldn't do anything wrong."

"During those early days our dressing room was a madhouse. Fans stormed the runway carrying armloads of food, mostly bratwurst and other varieties of sausages, as they fought their way past the guards at the door. An ice cream company installed a freezer, jamming it to the top each day," Charlie Grimm remembered.

Everyone on the Braves' bench enjoyed the spoils of being part of Milwaukee's new royal family; at the time sportswriter Al Hirshberg estimated that the Braves individually profited by more than $100,000 by Milwaukee's generosity. Local car dealer Wally Rank offered each player the use of a brand-new car. A group of fans helped Billy Bruton find a three-room apartment in Milwaukee and arranged for a store to lend him furniture, at no charge, through the end of the season. The local Jewish community sponsored a night to honor Sid Gordon. Iowans hosted a night for native son Jack Dittmer. The Federation of German-American Societies provided Warren Spahn a $5,000 tractor for use on his five hundred–acre farm in Oklahoma. African Americans honored Jim Pendleton, George Crowe, and Billy Bruton. Even utility man Sibby Sisti received a $1,000 bond, assorted gifts, and four bicycles for his children during a night in his honor.

For one player the accolades may have been too much. On June 16, thirty-five thousand fans sang "Happy Birthday" when the Polish community hosted a party at

> "Every day is Christmas for us. Milwaukee is out of this world."
> —MAX SURKONT

home plate for Max Surkont. Surkont received a large amount of his favorite food, Polish sausage—and proceeded to eat it like there was no tomorrow. "It surely was no coincidence that he was 9–1 up to the sausage barrage and 2–4 the rest of the season," Braves historian Gary Caruso wrote in *The Braves Encyclopedia*. "He was traded during the winter and never had another winning season."

For most, though, the honors inspired their performance on the field. During Andy Pafko's twenty-game hitting streak in August, Lutherans turned out ten thousand strong on August 21 to honor the outfielder. "They had an Andy Pafko night and they gave me a Cadillac," the Boyceville, Wisconsin, native fondly recollected. Then, on September 26, Blatz Brewing Company proclaimed Pafko the winner of its "Best of the Braves" contest. "I thought that I didn't have a chance," he remembered in an interview years later. "I mean, we had guys like Mathews, Spahn, Crandall, and Logan. But do you know, I won the most popular player contest that year, because the fans of Wisconsin loved me. They voted for me, so I won a Chevrolet. That to me was a big, big thrill."

As wonderful as the gifts and admiration were during an era when a player's minimum salary was $7,500, Pafko and the other Braves became average Joes at season's end. "I always had a winter job," Pafko recalled. "I worked for the Miller Brewing Company one year in Milwaukee. Then I worked for the Coca-Cola Company as a public relations man." Along with some off-season income, employment provided the Braves an opportunity to promote themselves throughout the community and interact with fans on a personal level.

"They gave us everything," shortstop Johnny Logan said of the fans' unbridled loyalty. "But us ballplayers had to reciprocate. And every night in winter we would go out to these 'sports nights' in all these churches—Catholic, Protestant, Lutheran, Jewish. We had a desire to play the game, promote ourselves and be liked by the city of Milwaukee."

For those fans who couldn't meet the Braves in person at social events or get tickets to the games at County Stadium, the radio was the closest they could get to participating in one of the biggest parties in baseball history. Regardless of where you were during the summer of 1953 in Milwaukee, the Braves were the soundtrack to the city's sentimental soul. From corner taverns, filling stations, department stores, and ice cream fountains to neighborhood porches and parks, the exuberant calls from the team's play-by-play announcer, Earl Gillespie, complemented the events of everyday life.

With the 1953 season at its midpoint, Milwaukee continued to flirt with first place, proving its early season success wasn't a fluke. "At the end of June we were in second place, half a game behind the Dodgers. By now I was convinced that the Braves had started to jell. We had won 42 and lost 27," Charlie Grimm recalled.

> **"We had a desire to play the game, promote ourselves and be liked by the city of Milwaukee."**
> —JOHNNY LOGAN

FACING PAGE: Capitalizing on the players' newfound celebrity in Milwaukee, many local businesses approached them about endorsing products and services. (DAVID KLUG COLLECTION)

STAR RIGHT FIELDER
OF THE MILWAUKEE BRAVES
ANDY PAFKO

Braves radio announcers Earl Gillespie (left) and Blaine Walsh (right). For eleven years, Earl Gillespie's microphone for the Braves' flagship radio station, WEMP, would be the conduit for millions of fans across the Midwest to the excitement and drama brewing wherever the Braves were taking the field. In a unique strategy, the Braves allowed games to be broadcast simultaneously on WEMP and its competing Milwaukee radio station, WTMJ, due to WTMJ's stronger signal. To satisfy the managements of both stations, Gillespie shared the microphone during portions of each game with WTMJ's Blaine Walsh. (LEFT: DAVID KLUG COLLECTION; RIGHT: ROBERT KOEHLER COLLECTION)

One of the most valuable pieces of the Braves lineup began showcasing his natural slugging ability in St. Louis on July 12. While going four-for-five in the first game of a doubleheader sweep of the Cardinals, Eddie Mathews connected on his first major-league grand slam—the first in Milwaukee Braves history. The hard-hitting third baseman's remarkable physique, powerful stroke, and bat speed impressed even his manager. "Mathews hits the ball later than anyone but Ted Williams," Grimm gloated to the press. "He lets the ball break right on top of him. Then, whammo! It's the wrists that do it."

Arriving in Milwaukee already labeled as a potential all-time great, Mathews struggled to keep a low profile around town. Because he was the focus of unwavering fan adulation, at times it took him an hour to reach his car after home games. Mathews's hero status in Milwaukee was never more evident than when he fouled off a line drive in the County Stadium stands that accidentally struck a fan and knocked him unconscious. The Braves were worried about the negative press and potential lawsuits. But when the fan regained consciousness, with the seams of the ball imprinted on his forehead, his first groggy words were, "Do you think Mathews would autograph the ball?"

Baseball was taking notice of the emerging Braves, and Warren Spahn, Del Crandall, and Eddie Mathews were named to the 1953 All-Star squad. On July 14, the National League bested its American League rivals 5–1, with Mathews scoring the senior circuit's first run and Spahn hurling three strong innings to get credit for the win.

When Warren Spahn began taking the mound in Milwaukee, he was already regarded as one of the game's finest pitchers. Born in Buffalo, New York, Spahn had entered high school as a first baseman but quickly switched to pitching when he realized the team already had an all-city player at the position. His meticulous control and dominating fastball caught the attention of a Boston Braves scout. After signing

In 1953 Eddie Mathews led the National League with forty-seven home runs.
(WHI IMAGE ID 49249)

with the Braves in 1940 for eighty dollars a month, he left to serve in the army for three years during World War II. He returned to baseball in 1946 and quickly established himself as one of baseball's most competitive mound masters.

During the Braves' 1948 pennant drive, Warren Spahn and fellow pitcher Johnny Sain inspired *Boston Post* sports editor Gerald Hern to write a verse that became one of the more famous verbal gems in sports: "First we'll use Spahn, then we'll use Sain, Then an off day, followed by rain. Back will come Spahn, followed by Sain, And followed, we hope, by two days of rain." Despite the poetic call to arms, the Braves lost the 1948 World Series to the Cleveland Indians.

Already considered to be entering the twilight of his career by 1953, the Braves' most seasoned warrior had thrown a commanding two-hitter against the Pirates on June 23 only to lose the game. Many thought his best performance of the season had been in vain, but on the first day of August the Braves sent Spahn to the mound in hopes of getting one step closer to catching the first-place Dodgers.

Waging a battle against the Philadelphia Phillies in Milwaukee, the southpaw flirted with pitching immortality: a perfect game. Spahn's specialty—a good fastball backed up by a slow curve—made Philadelphia's lineup look helpless and led the Braves to a 5–0 win. If not for Richie Ashburn's infield single in the fourth inning,

Warren Spahn's twenty-three victories and 2.10 ERA were both National League bests in 1953.
(WHI IMAGE ID 6224)

Spahn's thirty-first career shutout would have also been an elusive perfect game.

But as masterful as Spahn was against Philadelphia, he was unable to continue his bat-stifling ways. Following a 4–3 loss to the Dodgers on August 6, his seventh straight defeat against Brooklyn dating back to 1951, Spahn tried to explain his ineffectiveness. "It isn't just that the Dodgers have so many right-handed hitters that makes them tough," he was quoted in *Milwaukee's Miracle Braves*, "it's that they're an experienced ball club. They run well, make no mistakes and take advantage of any mistakes you make."

As the Dodgers continued to play near-perfect baseball and expand their lead in the standings, Milwaukee refused to fold. During a doubleheader at Pittsburgh's Forbes Field on August 30, the Braves engaged in a power surge never before witnessed on a major-league baseball diamond. In the first game, Milwaukee hitters clubbed eight home runs for a new National League record. Outfielder Jim Pendleton became the second rookie in history to hit three home runs in one game, while Eddie Mathews (the first rookie to hit three homers in a game, just a year earlier) hit two round-trippers. Logan, Crandall, and Dittmer each connected for one apiece in the Braves' lopsided 19–4 victory. In the second game Mathews, Adcock, Logan, and Sid Gordon each added homers during the Braves 11–5 defeat of the Pirates, giving the Braves a total of 12 homers and setting a National League record for the most home runs in a doubleheader.

Thanks in large part to their late-season slugging, the Braves continued to hold on to second place through the end of August. With their efforts tallied at the box office after every home game, Milwaukee proved itself worthy of being a major-league city. By September 4 County Stadium's attendance eclipsed the 1948 Boston Braves' National League pennant–winning figures. With a month of the season still remaining, the *Milwaukee Journal* challenged the Braves to top the greatest attendance giant the National League had ever seen: the Brooklyn Dodgers, who in 1947 pulled in an astronomical 1,807,439 fans.

Joe Adcock, Sid Gordon, Eddie Mathews, Andy Pafko, and Billy Bruton helped the Braves establish a franchise record of 156 round-trippers in 1953. (ALL-AMERICAN SPORTS, LLC)

Admission into Milwaukee County Stadium in '53 was the hottest ticket in town. (ROBERT KOEHLER COLLECTION)

> "They talk about other cities like Milwaukee. It just can't be."
>
> –JOHN QUINN

As the Braves lunged toward the Dodgers' 1947 attendance record, they failed to catch their 1953 counterparts in the standings. Although they looked like pennant contenders through the All-Star break, Grimm's team couldn't keep pace. On September 12 the Braves watched Brooklyn clinch its second straight pennant with a 5–2 verdict in Milwaukee—the earliest any team had ever accomplished the feat.

With their first season in Milwaukee drawing to a close, the Braves focused on making history during their home finale on September 20. After losing the first game of a doubleheader to the Cincinnati Redlegs 5–3, Charlie Grimm sent rookie Joey Jay to start on the mound for the nightcap—making the eighteen-year-old hurler the first former Little Leaguer to appear in a major-league game. Although the game was called after six and a half innings due to darkness, Jay gave up only three hits while earning the 3–0 victory.

More significantly, the doubleheader brought the Braves' total season attendance to 1,826,397 patrons, a new National League record. During their seventy-seven home games, the Braves drew more than twice Milwaukee's metropolitan population and maintained an 80 percent capacity at County Stadium with an average of 23,719 spectators per game. Because the Braves' relocation had been made public only a month before the start of the 1953 season, they achieved the record with literally no off-season promotional efforts toward ticket sales. "They talk about other cities like Milwaukee," general manager John Quinn said. "It just can't be. You have to have a spontaneous reaction. That's what we've had here. The people really wanted major league baseball."

Finishing with a 92–62 record, thirteen games behind the Dodgers, the Braves credited the season-long support from the fans for their turnaround in the standings. "The same club that finished seventh in Boston finished second in Milwaukee," Braves public relations director Donald Davidson noted. "If the difference wasn't in the enthusiasm of the crowd, then what was it?"

With the fans' season-long loyalty and enthusiasm sparking the team from cellar dwellers to pennant contenders, Lou Perini's gamble had paid off handsomely. The construction tycoon who purchased the Braves with a fortune made building roads, airports, and ammunition dumps approached America's Pastime no differently. "Lack of baseball experience is an advantage," Perini told reporters. "We take a sound business approach to the game. As contractors, we are planners and we know that a good organization will accomplish wonders."

With the franchise netting nearly $1.5 million in profits, Perini's decision to move the Braves from Boston to Milwaukee led to one of the greatest success stories in baseball history. Looking to share the wealth, Perini voluntarily amended the Braves' contract with County Stadium, paying a combined rent of $250,000 for the 1953 and 1954 seasons instead of the previously agreed upon $1,000 per season. Perini's generously providing the Milwaukee County treasury with $249,000 more than its original lease called for earned him a hefty chunk of goodwill among Milwaukee elders. Probably the only member of the Braves who lost money in 1953 thanks to the Braves' attendance figures was Warren Spahn. While negotiating his contract following the 1952 season, he had scoffed at management's offer of a commission once the Boston Braves reached the 800,000-fan threshold. Based on their less-than-stellar performance of 281,000 fans in 1952, he took a $25,000 guarantee instead. When the Braves drew 1,826,397 fans in Milwaukee, Spahn's decision essentially cost him $102,639.70.

Milwaukee's dazzling performance at the gate proved it was capable of being a "big-league" city in every sense of the term. Beyond

The Braves' quest to break the National League attendance record in 1953 became a statewide effort. (MILWAUKEE JOURNAL SENTINEL)

The Braves brought a sense of pride to the entire state of Wisconsin. (DAVID KLUG COLLECTION)

the Braves' box office receipts, city officials estimated that the team's arrival generated nearly $5 million in new business in Milwaukee. The intangible rewards of hosting the major-league franchise were even greater, as every business and industry seemed to benefit in some way. "I don't think there was ever a team that did more for a city than the Braves did for Milwaukee," future baseball commissioner Bud Selig once remarked. "And it worked both ways."

> **"I don't think there was ever a team that did more for a city than the Braves did for Milwaukee."**
> **–BUD SELIG**

"It took the Yankees half a century to build their championship spirit," Andy Pafko told the press. "Something quite similar was born overnight in Wisconsin's largest city. Within a single season the Braves captured the same feeling that a fellow must get playing football for Notre Dame . . . or wearing a Marine uniform." Milwaukee quickly capitalized on the Braves' success and the fans' enthusiasm to brand itself major-league worthy. The city made numerous improvements, some necessary, some window dressing, simply because the Braves now belonged to Milwaukee. Plans for a new freeway, which had been on the drawing board for years, finally crystallized, and a new public library, stymied for years because of the expense, was suddenly voted into existence.

Even National League president Warren Giles, who was initially skeptical of the Braves' proposed relocation to Milwaukee, advised owners that Perini's success proved that "there are new fields of operation which are fertile."

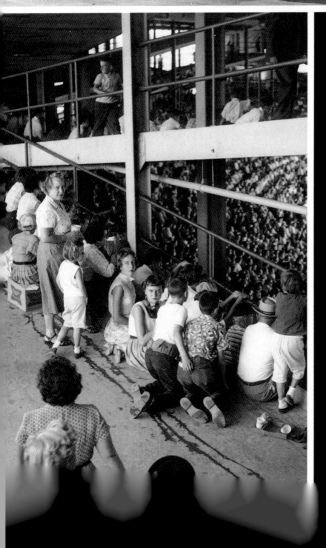

ABOVE, LEFT: Charged with building interest among potential fans was the Braves' goodwill ambassador, Hal Goodnough. During his first two and a half years on the job, the former schoolmaster drove more than sixty-three thousand miles and made more than 650 speeches to groups across Wisconsin, from kindergarten classes, bankers' groups, churches, and nursing homes to state prisons. (ROBERT KOEHLER COLLECTION)

ABOVE, RIGHT: Braves boosters were some of the most enthusiastic and dedicated in all of baseball. (ROBERT KOEHLER COLLECTION)

LEFT: The Braves introduced the major leagues' first Girls' Knot Hole Club during the 1954 season. (ROBERT KOEHLER COLLECTION)

RIGHT: The Milwaukee Braves organization was groundbreaking in its marketing of baseball to women. (DAVID KLUG COLLECTION)

The day after Adcock's record-breaking performance, the Braves routed the Dodgers again. To silence the Braves' offensive juggernaut, Brooklyn's Clem Labine bounced a fastball off Adcock's head in the fourth inning. "There was no fight, but Adcock would have been seriously injured if he had not been wearing his batting helmet," Donald Davidson recalled in *Caught Short*. "Joe's protective headgear was split in two by Labine's pitch." Adcock was carried from the field, his bat finally silenced. In the bottom of the sixth, the Braves' Gene Conley reciprocated by knocking down Jackie Robinson, who in turn ended up scrapping with Eddie Mathews. In the end, the Braves clinched their tenth win in a row with a 10–5 victory—Conley's ninth straight win.

Having won twenty of twenty-two, the Braves were within a mere three and a half games of the top by August 15. "Despite some ups and downs, the Braves fully expected to be playing in the World Series that season," Eddie Mathews noted in his autobiography, *Eddie Mathews and the National Pastime*.

On July 31, 1954, Joe Adcock saw just seven pitches in his five at bats while clobbering four home runs against the Dodgers. (DAVID KLUG COLLECTION)

As the Braves continued to rise in the standings, Mathews and the "Milwaukee Miracle" were featured on the inaugural cover of *Sports Illustrated* on August 16, 1954. "The photographer said he took about 150 shots of different players and turned them all over to the editor," Mathews recalled. "The editor chose that particular photograph because he said it was timeless—you don't really see anybody's face, and it doesn't emphasize an individual, but rather a scene that's repeated thousands and thousands of times every year."

It was a natural choice for the upstart magazine, since at the time most considered Mathews to be the greatest threat to break Babe Ruth's all-time home-run record. "If anybody can do it I'd say Eddie has the chance," Grimm told reporters. "He has a fine disposition, he does nothing to impair his great physical condition and I believe he has remained unspoiled by all the hero worship that has come his way in Milwaukee."

Admired as much for his All-American looks as his athletic ability, Mathews never sought out the spotlight, even as a stellar high school running back in Santa Barbara, California. Although he was approached by several colleges offering football scholarships, Mathews signed with the Braves after they offered him a $6,000 guaranteed contract. Mathews felt the guaranteed money would immediately benefit his family. When he reached Milwaukee, he continued to reluctantly avoid the spotlight. His reputation as a tough interview quickly spread. "What can a guy like me tell them that would be worth printing?" Mathews asked. "I'll try to answer their questions, but they've got to realize that baseball comes first with me. I'm not the most pleasant guy to be around after I've gone 0-for-4."

"I'm not the most pleasant guy to be around after I've gone 0-for-4."

—EDDIE MATHEWS

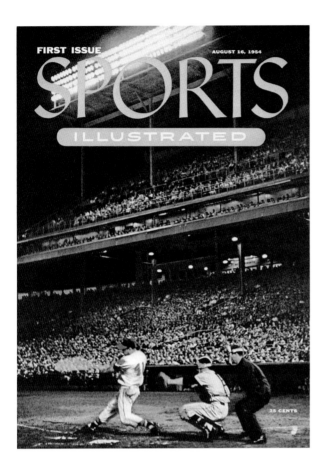

ABOVE: Braves third baseman Eddie Mathews graced the inaugural *Sports Illustrated* cover on August 16, 1954. (SPORTS ILLUSTRATED)

RIGHT: Eddie Mathews grew increasingly disenchanted with the attention he received as a superstar in Milwaukee. (DAVID KLUG COLLECTION)

But as a shy and otherwise introverted athlete, Mathews grew increasingly uncomfortable with the prediction that he would be heir to Ruth's crown. "What everybody seems to forget," Quinn scolded reporters, "is that when they're dealing with Mathews, they're dealing with a boy. Here he is 23 years old and he's already been in the major leagues three seasons."

At first Mathews regarded the flood of attention with affectionate amusement, but eventually it began to wear on him. Wherever he went in Milwaukee, admirers hovered. He couldn't eat, watch a movie, or walk around a street corner without being ambushed with an autograph request. "Why, I've known him to stay in the clubhouse for two hours after a game trying to escape the crowd of fans," Braves coach Bucky Walters told the *Street & Smith Baseball Yearbook* in 1954. "But they're always waiting for him, especially the girls. Gosh, how those gals go for him!"

Mathews lost his fun-loving attitude, even toward the same writers and fans who had helped coronate him as the king of Milwaukee. He began avoiding the public and found solace in nightclubs and alcohol. "Mathews liked to have a good time and was probably the hardest-living guy on the team," Henry Aaron wrote in his autobiography *I Had a Hammer: The Hank Aaron Story*. "I didn't go out with Mathews very often because you never knew what might happen." That summer, Mathews's off-the-field exploits jumped from the sports section onto the front pages of the Milwaukee newspapers. A story chronicled Mathews's arrest in the early morning hours for speeding, running a traffic light, and giving a Wauwatosa traffic cop a hard time. Although the charge was presented in court as nothing more than a speeding violation, Mathews's reputation had been tarnished. Fined fifty dollars by the court and another one hundred dollars by manager Charlie Grimm, the Braves slugger realized the effect on his checkbook was minimal compared to the shower of disappointment from reporters and fans. While the incident was one of the most important steps in Mathews's process of growing up, it also hardened his resolve to keep his private life out of the spotlight.

Despite his lack of interest in speaking with reporters, Mathews won over many of the Braves veterans with his dedication on the diamond. "Eddie came to play every day. He never missed a ballgame," Warren Spahn asserted. "I was with the Braves when Eddie came up in '52, and he couldn't stop a ground ball. He worked every day until he became a good fielder."

Following his appearance on the cover of *Sports Illustrated*, Mathews had the dubious distinction of being the first victim of the "*Sports Illustrated* jinx"—a long succession of athletes have inexplicably been injured, lost the big game, or endured lackluster performances after appearing on the magazine's cover. During a game against the Cubs on August 22, Mathews was hit on the hand by pitcher Hal Jeffcoat. The injury required stitches and kept him out of the lineup for nearly two weeks. "The ball jammed my middle finger against the bat and split the finger wide open," Mathews remembered. "It bled like a stuck pig."

On August 29 the Dodgers swept the Braves in a doubleheader. But County Stadium's crowd of 45,922 fans brought the season's total to 1,841,666, a new National League record. "At the end of August we had already hustled more customers into the stadium than during the entire first season," Charlie Grimm noted. Building on the tremendous statewide interest, the Braves created eleven ticket agencies in Wisconsin cities within a hundred-mile radius of Milwaukee that had populations in excess of twenty-five thousand. "The Braves had made it easier for the outlying fans to buy the precious tickets, setting up branch offices in Fond du Lac, Oshkosh, Appleton, Racine, Kenosha, Madison, Beloit, Janesville, Sheboygan, Manitowoc and Green Bay," Grimm recounted in *Jolly Cholly's Story*. County Stadium's encore performance at the ticket turnstiles proved that Milwaukee's honeymoon with the team wasn't a one-year affair. When the final figures were tabulated at the end of the 1954 season, a grand total of 2,131,388 fans had witnessed the "Milwaukee Miracle."

Nobody relished Milwaukee's success more than the Braves' forty-eight-inch-tall publicity director, Donald Davidson. Davidson had grown up around the game, serving as a mascot, batboy, and press box attendant in Boston. After moving up to the Braves' front office in 1948, Davidson spent most of his career as the team's publicity director and later as its traveling secretary. "Donald was tough. He really demanded respect and he got it," Mathews recalled. While his size got him noticed in a crowd, it was his personality that made him one of baseball's most colorful front-office personalities. "He would swear a blue streak at us. God, he could cuss. Even for baseball, his language was exceptional," Mathews said.

Since County Stadium was often sold out, the Braves encouraged patients at the National Soldiers Home Veterans Administration Hospital to watch games from sloping Mockingbird Hill, which overlooked right field. (ROBERT KOEHLER COLLECTION)

BELOW: Braves pitcher Gene Conley and publicity director Donald Davidson (DAVID KLUG COLLECTION)

As publicity director in 1954, Davidson decided that "Hank" sounded more "personable" than Henry when referring to the team's shy rookie tearing up National League pitching. Davidson was also responsible for assigning Aaron one of the most recognizable numbers in baseball history. According to Aaron's biography *Aaron*, he was originally assigned the number 5 upon signing up with the Braves. When he requested a double-digit jersey, Davidson replied to the request with a sarcastic, "Like what? You're so skinny, I don't know how a little bastard like you could carry two numbers around."

"I don't mean just any kind of double number. I mean like 22, 33, or 44, something like that," Aaron replied.

Davidson retorted, "Henry, dammit, don't you know that all the great ones were single numbers? Babe Ruth was number 3, Lou Gehrig was number [4]. Joe DiMaggio was number 9. Stan Musial is number 6. Ted Williams is number 9. Mickey Mantle is number 7. And you want to carry two numbers around?"

But by Labor Day weekend, Aaron's jersey request was temporarily forgotten while Milwaukee focused on overtaking the first-place Giants. The Braves arrived in Cincinnati still capable of clinching the pennant. "Our dugout was alive and you had that

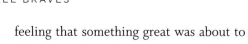

feeling that something great was about to happen to this ball club," Aaron recalled. "We were still in the pennant race. We were just five games back of the Giants, who were leading and right on the Dodgers' tails."

The Braves won the first game of the September 5 doubleheader 11–8. Aaron led the charge in the second game. After he smacked a screaming line drive into center field, the Braves rookie looked to make his fifth hit of the day a triple. Rounding second base, he hit the dirt and broke his ankle sliding into third. "You'll never guess who came in to run for me—Bobby Thomson himself. Bobby begins the season in the hospital and I take his job and I end the season in the hospital and he gets his job back," Aaron said. "By this time, though, I knew something I didn't know when Bobby went to the hospital. I knew I could play in the big leagues."

The Braves went on to sweep the Redlegs, dominate the Cubs, and pound the Pirates to secure their third ten-game winning streak of the season. With just four games separating them from the National League–leading New York Giants on September 10, the Braves traveled to Brooklyn for another heated late-season series. "Whenever we played the Dodgers, somebody got knocked down or beaned or words were exchanged," Mathews remembered.

Although Milwaukee lost the opener, Joe Adcock connected for his ninth round-tripper in Ebbets Field that season—tying the major-league mark for the most homers in an opposing park in one year. During twenty-two games against the Dodgers in 1954, Adcock had batted .395, with thirty-two hits, nine homers, and twenty-two RBIs. Tired of being terrorized, the Dodgers' pitching staff was desperate to silence the Braves' bats. "See, in those days, we had knockdowns. If a batter was having a lot of success against a pitcher or against his team, the pitcher would knock him down. He wouldn't necessarily hit you, but he would throw inside or near your head," Eddie Mathews explained. "We pretty much accepted that fact."

The Dodgers' Don Newcombe snuffed out the remainder of the Braves' season with one pitch by breaking Adcock's wrist. With Aaron already lost for the season, the wheels came off the Braves offense, and they quietly faded into third place, eight games behind the champion Giants and three behind the Dodgers, with an 89–65 record.

Although the Braves had established themselves as legitimate pennant contenders, the first criticism of Charlie Grimm's relaxed and fun-loving managerial style arose from the team's disgruntled second baseman. "Danny [O'Connell] was an aggressive ball player who spoke his mind, but he was a long time blaming me for the Braves' failure to win the 1954 pennant. He said a lack of fighting spirit cost us the

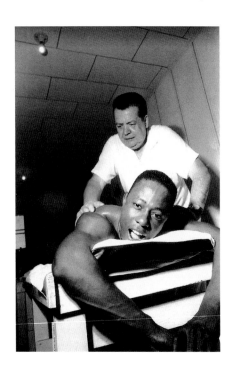

Despite sitting out nearly the entire last month of the 1954 season in an ankle cast, Henry Aaron still played in 122 games, collected 131 hits, belted 13 home runs, and drove home 69 runs with a solid .280 batting average. (WHI IMAGE ID 26384)

Jack Dittmer (tagging out Brooklyn's Jackie Robinson at second base) was part of Milwaukee's league-leading defensive unit in 1954. (ROBERT KOEHLER COLLECTION)

flag," Grimm remembered. "That's O'Connell's version. It's his privilege if he wants to pop off. And it won't make me change my system of managing. I think I'm aggressive in my own way. And I think our team was that way on the field."

Suffering from an injury-plagued roster all season combined with a slow start in April, Milwaukee still featured one of the top offenses, defenses, and pitching staffs in baseball during the 1954 season. "We didn't win the pennant," Aaron said. "But the Braves' time was coming. We were all going to grow a little bit each season. A pennant wasn't far off."

> "I think I'm agressive in my own way. And I think our team was that way on the field."
> —CHARLIE GRIMM

◆ ◆ ◆

During the off-season, the franchise lost its number one booster when brewery mogul Frederick Miller's airplane crashed and burned shortly after taking off from Milwaukee's Billy Mitchell Airport. Miller, his twenty-year-old son Fred Jr., and two pilots employed by Miller Brewing Company had been on their way to a hunting cabin in Canada; all four were killed. With Miller's untimely death, Wisconsin was without one of its most generous residents. "As a businessman Mr. Miller obviously recognized the advertising potential that sports held for his product, but his interest in sports went far beyond that," Eddie Mathews recalled. "When the Green Bay Packers were threatened with bankruptcy in the early '50s, he bought stock and sponsored radio broadcasts and helped sell tickets."

Some observers thought that, as a personal and professional confidant of Lou Perini, Miller might have had a larger role in the Braves' future. "Before his death there was a lot of conversation that Miller might buy out Perini. Who knows, had Miller lived, the Braves might still be in Milwaukee," Charlie Grimm speculated in his 1968 memoir.

With heavy hearts, several Braves players reported to camp before the approved March 1 starting date, looking to build on their previous season's third-place finish. "I still needed some hard work to get in shape after having the cast on all winter, so, at John Quinn's request, I reported early to Bradenton," Hank Aaron recalled. "After I was there a day or so, I got a telegram from the commissioner, Ford Frick, telling me I was fined for reporting early."

Ford Frick's five hundred dollar fine wasn't the only thing Aaron found hanging in his locker. There was also a tomahawk-clad double-digit jersey with the number 44 on the back. Despite his ribbing of Aaron, Donald Davidson fondly recalled in his autobiography *Caught Short* that "four times in his career he hit 44 home runs, and I regret that I did not give him number 70."

By the end of spring training, prognosticators felt the Braves had the earmarks of a scrappy pennant contender—youth blended with experience, a combination Grimm hoped to craft into a pennant winner. "In our plans for 1955, we were trying to fit in the pieces that would give the doting fans their just reward," he explained.

Milwaukee County Stadium's turnstiles clicked at a record pace for the 1955 home opener, as 43,640 enthusiastic fans broke a National League Opening Day attendance record. The electrified crowd in full Braves regalia bought baseball caps at $2, T-shirts for $1, team jackets at $6.95, and official uniforms for $7.95 at the novelty stands throughout the ballpark.

On the diamond, Milwaukee's Warren Spahn dueled against Cincinnati's Gerry Staley. With the Braves trailing 2–1 in the bottom of the eighth inning, rookie Chuck Tanner went in to pinch hit for Spahn. Making his major-league debut, Tanner refused to waste any swings at the plate and proceeded to blast Staley's first pitch into the right-field bleachers. Tanner's round-tripper tied the score at two and ignited the Braves. They tallied another pair of runs later in the inning to clinch the 4–2 win over the Redlegs for the dramatic Opening Day finish.

The remainder of April found the Braves mired between fourth and fifth place due to their slow start and inconsistent play. Meanwhile, the Dodgers started their season with ten straight wins. By

The Milwaukee Braves' 1955 Opening Day lineup featured (from left to right) Billy Bruton, Danny O'Connell, Eddie Mathews, Andy Pafko, Henry Aaron, Joe Adcock, Johnny Logan, Del Crandall, and Bob Buhl (not pictured). (ROBERT KOEHLER COLLECTION)

On April 20, 1955, right-hander Humberto Robinson debuted with the Braves, the first native of Panama to reach the majors. (DAVID KLUG COLLECTION)

a long-term basis," Lou Perini told reporters, "there may be some leveling off in attendance. But it is not a novelty. There is a real, wholesome enthusiasm for baseball and fewer distractions in Milwaukee and the state."

Despite the slight dip in attendance in 1955, County Stadium had nearly six million paid admissions over its first three seasons. The county collected approximately $471,000 in revenue from gate and concession receipts during that time. The stadium's ample parking lots alone earned the county more than $500,000 between '53 and '55. In total, Milwaukee County grossed over $1,078,000 during County Stadium's first three years of operation. The contract between the club and county also stipulated that the county receive a payment of 5 percent of gate and concession receipts, which in 1955 amounted to $195,989.91. Such prosperity in a city whose metropolitan population was only 871,047 left every baseball owner pondering the prospects of franchise relocation.

There was plenty of music aboard the Braves Booster Club train that traveled on a ten-day tour of New York, Philadelphia, and Brooklyn to support the team. (MILWAUKEE JOURNAL SENTINEL)

As the season concluded, Milwaukee shook off the 1954 world champion New York Giants to settle for second place a distant thirteen and a half games behind Brooklyn, with a respectable 85–69 record. "Aaron and Mathews had great years, but they couldn't carry the load," Grimm said. "When the season started, I thought we had the best pitching, the best infield, and the best outfield in the league. Statistics proved otherwise."

As critics began to question if the Braves would ever seriously contend for a pennant, even Grimm noticed the public's optimism beginning to waver. "I thought the notices were a bit premature, though I had been around long enough to realize that the manager is the sacrificial lamb when the public starts wondering what's holding back the team," he said. "By this time, in the third season in Milwaukee, the fans were becoming impatient for a pennant."

◆ ◆ ◆

The Braves' 1956 spring training camp atmosphere was clouded with doubt from the start. Labeled an enigma by baseball prognosticators, Milwaukee was expected to finally overcome injuries that had overshadowed its potential in seasons past. After three bittersweet years for the Braves in Milwaukee, critics boldly declared that the fate of manager Charlie Grimm rested on the team's ability to clinch a pennant. Although his club had finished second, third, and second, respectively, in his three seasons at the helm in Milwaukee, Grimm's managerial style was increasingly criticized. "He gave players a free rein, feeling that they were professionals who would not take advantage of him. Unfortunately, it doesn't work that way. Charlie knew the game, but he was too lenient with the Braves," Donald Davidson noted in *Caught Short*.

During spring training, Grimm maintained his theory that players make the successful manager, but he adjusted his once-conservative and predictable management style around the Braves' emerging strengths: speed, pitching, and power. "When the 1956 season opened, I was confident we would go all the way," Grimm remarked.

It seemed that as long as everyone stayed healthy, the Milwaukee Braves' new All-Star-filled lineup couldn't miss winning the pennant. Their hitting attack, anchored by Henry Aaron, Joe Adcock, and Eddie Mathews, was one of the most fearsome middle-of-the-lineup alignments in all of baseball. Their ageless wonder, Warren Spahn, looked to continue dominating National League

Charlie Grimm offered cigars to pitchers Phil Paine, Carlton Willey, and Lou Burdette during 1956 spring training. (ROBERT KOEHLER COLLECTION)

After finishing their daily spring training workouts, Braves (from left to right) Red Murff, Del Rice, Dave Jolly, and Sam Taylor pooled their efforts at a Bradenton billiards parlor. (MILWAUKEE JOURNAL SENTINEL)

hitters, while Bob Buhl was expected to fully rebound from an injury that had shortened his 1954 season. To ensure that the Braves played up to expectations, Perini appointed former Pittsburgh Pirates manager Fred Haney to Grimm's coaching staff. "Certainly, Haney was there as a backup. He had managerial experience with a couple of teams in the big leagues," Milwaukee Braves' historian Bob Buege recalled.

Back in Milwaukee, loyal Braves fans were eager to dethrone the National League juggernauts, and more than 900,000 tickets were sold before Opening Day. "Expectations were high for the Braves in 1956, both our own and the fans.' We thought we had as good a team as Brooklyn, or better," Eddie Mathews declared.

At the April 17 home opener, 39,766 fans watched Lou Burdette shut out the Cubs 6–0. Behind the pitching talents of Spahn, Burdette, and Buhl, Milwaukee won its first three games en route to nine of its first twelve. By the beginning of May, Grimm's Braves had claimed first place after holding off the rest of the National League for nearly a month and boasted a 19–10 record.

Although they were performing at an exceptional level, the Braves couldn't separate themselves from the rest of the National League. With no team trailing first place by more than three and a half games, the 1956 pennant race quickly shaped up as one of the most exciting in National League history. No team could establish itself as a clear favorite, and the Braves, Dodgers, Redlegs, Cardinals, and Pirates all were battling for first into June. The pressure continued to mount on Milwaukee, fueled by New York writer Milton Richman, who predicted that "Charlie Grimm will have the Milwaukee Braves in first place by June 15, or he'll be out of work."

Questions surrounded the Braves' pennant aspirations in 1956. (UWM LIBRARIES, ARCHIVES DEPARTMENT RAINOVIC COLLECTION IMAGE 139)

Knocked off the top of the standings in early June by the Pirates, Milwaukee went on to drop nine of thirteen games—and ended up reeling in fifth place at 24–22. By June 16 word of a management change began to spread among the players. "Before the game started against the Dodgers in Brooklyn, I sensed that something was in the air," Grimm recalled. "The Perinis and other club officials were sitting in a box next to our dugout and newspapermen were interviewing them like mad. I was trying to pay strict attention to the action after the game started, but it didn't escape me that the players were whispering among each other on the bench."

Two days later the Braves dropped a 3–2 decision to the Dodgers after allowing two unearned runs and an eighth-inning home run to Duke Snider. Following the frustrating loss, Grimm resigned. "I've decided to let someone else take a crack at the job," Grimm told reporters at the press conference. "Anyone who can win ten or eleven in a row can win this thing."

In frigid February temperatures, Braves fans came well prepared with blankets and supplies to keep comfortable and warm while waiting more than two days outside County Stadium for 1956 season tickets to go on sale. (MILWAUKEE JOURNAL SENTINEL)

Frustrated with the Braves' underachievement in the standings, Perini replaced Grimm with Fred Haney. Haney fully realized the difficult situation he had inherited. "This is the toughest job I've ever faced. I mean it!" he commented to reporters. "These fellows are spoiled rotten. When you take a team to spring training, you can get things the way you think they ought to be. But in midseason you can only do so much; otherwise you may have something on your hands that you don't want. This situation can be worked out, but not overnight."

Haney had a reputation for being a good skipper with bad teams, having spent unsuccessful managing tours with the St. Louis Browns and Pittsburgh Pirates. While nobody knew if having Haney at the helm made the difference, or if Jolly Cholly's exit had served as the wakeup call, the Braves' performance began to take a turn. The Braves were in fifth place and four games out of first when Haney took the reins, but the club didn't stay there for long. "There is something magic about a change, though. I can't deny that," Aaron said. "We got cranked up again. All we needed was a kick in the britches."

Youngsters Michael Rodell and Thomas Greiner were left frustrated after a game at County Stadium was canceled due to inclement weather. (COURTESY OF MIKE RODELL)

During Haney's first game as skipper, Joe Adcock once again proved Ebbets Field was his favorite playground. He connected for three home runs, including a towering, game-winning homer in the ninth inning. "Sweeping the Dodgers that day gave us confidence, and all of a sudden we couldn't lose," Eddie Mathews said.

Milwaukee went on to win nine more games in a row before dropping a 4–2 decision to Robin Roberts on June 26 in Philadelphia. During their eleven consecutive victories, the Braves catapulted themselves from three and a half games out of first to a two-game lead over the rest of the National League. A reluctant Haney refused to

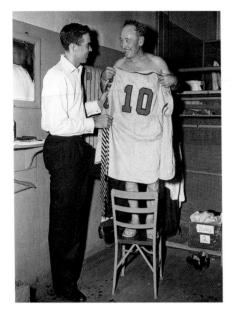

Fred Haney (right) held a number 10 jersey alongside pitcher Gene Conley to signify the Braves' tenth straight win since he took over as manager. (DAVID KLUG COLLECTION)

"Spahn and Burdette had been so good for so long that people didn't realize how much Buhl meant to us."

—HENRY AARON

take the credit. "Believe me, I'm no miracle man," he told reporters. "The Braves themselves deserve the credit for their winning streak. Don't give me any of it."

By the All-Star break Milwaukee cooled, and the pennant race became a tight three-team battle with only three games separating first from third. The Redlegs held the National League lead, with the Braves in second and the Dodgers right behind.

Baseball's twenty-third annual All-Star Game was held in Washington, D.C.'s Griffith Park. Four Braves were selected to the National League roster. The game featured an at bat by Henry Aaron and two innings pitched by Warren Spahn, who gave up the only three runs the American League scored in the Nationals' 7–3 victory. A slumping Eddie Mathews rode the pine, and catcher Del Crandall was replaced due to an injury. "I chipped some bones in my left elbow," the Braves' catcher recalled. "But it might have been a blessing in disguise. I had to cut down my swing as a result and maybe became a better hitter because of it."

In a thrilling second half of the season, the Braves won fifteen of their first seventeen games. The club's surge paralleled Joe Adcock's assault on opposing pitchers as he connected for ten home runs in thirteen consecutive games. So it was no surprise when on July 17 the Giants tried to slow him down the only way they knew how—by throwing at him. Ruben Gomez's first pitch in the second inning struck Adcock on the same wrist that had been broken a year earlier. "Joe started down to first base rubbing his bicep and mumbling to himself. About halfway there, Gomez for some reason started screaming at him. That just triggered Joe," Eddie Mathews recalled. "He was never going to start anything. But whatever Gomez said to him—it ticked him off because he charged the mound." Adcock's otherwise-easygoing persona boiled into an all-out rage. "When Joe charged the mound, Gomez cranked up and hit him again with the damn thing, harder than the first time but this time on the front of his thigh."

Adcock chased Gomez off the mound and into the Giants' clubhouse. "Gomez went in there and got an ice pick," Johnny Logan remembered. "The guys on his own team had to stop him." After the incident, both men were ejected, and the Braves eventually lost the game in twelve innings. Two days later Adcock followed up by continuing to pummel the Giants, this time with his bat. After driving in eight runs with a grand slam, a three-run homer, and an RBI single, he was finally taken out of the game after six innings in the 13–3 Braves win.

By the end of July, Milwaukee held a five-and-a-half-game lead. Behind the dynamite performances of Aaron, Adcock, and Mathews, the Braves established a major-league record on July 31 by hitting a home run in their twenty-second consecutive

The 1956 season found the Braves entangled in another highly contested National League pennant race. (UWM LIBRARIES, ARCHIVES DEPARTMENT RAINOVIC COLLECTION IMAGE 270)

game. The threesome's contrasting styles at the plate reflected their personalities. Aaron was the wrist hitter, with any pitch susceptible to being driven into play in an instant. Mathews was the stylist, his stance, swing, and coordination flirting with perfection. Adcock lacked both wrist action and stylistic panache, but his massive arms, swinging hips, and thrusting head generated awesome power.

Helping to hold the Braves' lead over Cincinnati and Brooklyn into August was a healthy Bob Buhl. "He was a nasty pitcher and a fierce competitor," Aaron observed. "Spahn and Burdette had been so good for so long that people didn't realize how much Buhl meant to us."

The Saginaw, Michigan, native had walked away from a pugilistic career after he knocked a boxing rival so cold he wasn't sure if his opponent would recover. "Until that happened," Buhl recounted, "I thought I might make boxing my career. But when I saw him lying on the canvas, out cold, I never wanted to see a boxing ring again." Buhl turned to baseball—and became one of the Braves' most potent arms. "When I joined the club," Braves backup catcher Del Rice told *Sport* magazine, "he was just a thrower. Now he's a real pitcher, the best in the league in my book. He's got a lot of good pitches—curve, slider and change-up, besides a fast one. He even throws a knuckler once in a while. He's got the batters looking for his fastball and he's fooling 'em with the other stuff."

The Dodger-slayer chalked up eight victories and a stifling 2.43 earned run average against the defending world champions in 1956. "Let's face it," Buhl admitted. "If you don't have luck, you can't win. You can pitch two-hitters and three-hitters until you're blue in the face and you'll still be a losing pitcher. Look at my record this year and you'll see what I mean. I'm just plain lucky."

In 1956 Henry Aaron (44) led the league in hits, doubles, and total bases and finished just one triple behind Billy Bruton. (ROBERT KOEHLER COLLECTION)

Bob Buhl finished with the second-highest winning percentage in the National League in 1956, with an 18–8 record. (UWM LIBRARIES, ARCHIVES DEPARTMENT RAINOVIC COLLECTION IMAGE 238)

But on August 4 in Pittsburgh, Buhl suffered a fractured finger when he was struck by a line drive. He pitched the final two months of the season in less than top condition and limped to an 18–8 record. With Buhl ailing, Milwaukee ventured to Philadelphia's historic Connie Mack Stadium for a crucial four-game series. After Henry Aaron knocked in the game-winning RBI in the thirteenth inning to secure the 3–2 victory in the first game of a doubleheader, Warren Spahn dueled Robin Roberts for twelve innings in the nightcap. Aaron hit another a game-winning RBI in the twelfth inning for the 4–3 victory.

The win was Spahn's two hundredth career victory, securing his place as the fifty-eighth pitcher to join the distinguished two hundred–wins club. At an age when most pitchers retired their worn-out arms, thirty-five-year-old Spahn continued to thrive on the mound with an unwavering will to win. After eleven seasons, his fastball was no longer as swift as it once was, but his control and patience continued to baffle enemy batsmen. As he often explained, "The more I pitched to a hitter, the less I was impressed by him."

Following a doubleheader sweep of the Phillies, the Braves dropped their next two games in Philadelphia and on September 15 fell out of first place by percentage points for the first time since July. For the rest of the month, the Braves were in and out of first place, but they went into the last three games of the season a full game ahead of the Brooklyn Dodgers. Milwaukee was in control of its own destiny as the pennant hung in the balance. "We had it. It was right there in our laps," Aaron said.

Needing to win only two of their last three games to guarantee at least a tie with the Dodgers for first place, Haney had his aces—Buhl, Spahn, and Burdette—lined up to pitch in St. Louis. But on September 28 the Cardinals trounced Buhl early en route to a 5–4 victory. With the Dodgers rained out in Pittsburgh that night, the Braves lead was down to half a game. Yet regardless of what Brooklyn did, the pennant was still Milwaukee's if they could win their final two games. The following day the Braves players were left to squirm in their hotel rooms as the Dodgers catapulted themselves into first place. "That was the key game," Aaron said. "You see, we went into it knowing that the Dodgers had taken a doubleheader from Pittsburgh that afternoon. The heat was on us."

> **"If you don't have luck, you can't win."**
>
> **–BOB BUHL**

In 1956 Bob Buhl, Warren Spahn, and Lou Burdette hurled eighteen, nineteen, and twenty wins, respectively, for the Braves. (ROBERT KOEHLER COLLECTION)

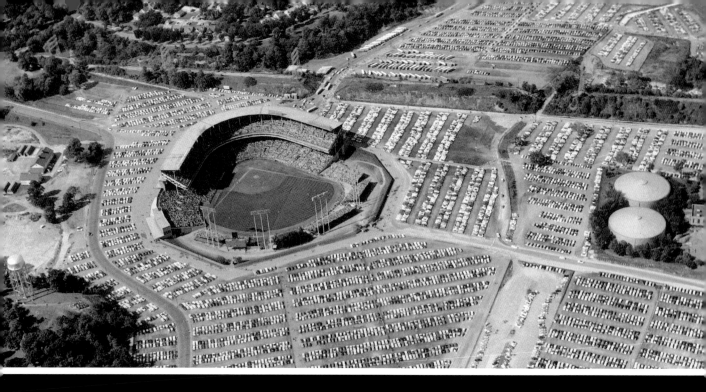

ABOVE: For the third consecutive season, the Braves drew more than two million fans to Milwaukee County Stadium in 1956. (COURTESY OF BOB BUEGE)

BELOW, LEFT: The Milwaukee Braves boosters supported the team during crucial road trips, including an August 1956 series against the Dodgers at Brooklyn's Ebbets Field. (DAVID KLUG COLLECTION)

BELOW, RIGHT: Despite losing two of their final three games and the 1956 pennant, the Braves and manager Fred Haney (in headdress) received a hero's welcome at General Mitchell Field upon the team's return from St. Louis. (WHI IMAGE ID 49354)

That night the Braves took the field confident they'd be back in first place, especially since their ace was looking to capture his twenty-first victory of the season. "Warren Spahn pitched his guts out in St. Louis," Henry Aaron recalled. "The Cards got only three hits in eleven innings."

> **"We had every reason to win, but it was like it wasn't meant to be."**
>
> —WARREN SPAHN

But with one out in the bottom of the twelfth, the Cardinals finally got to Spahn. After Stan Musial doubled and Ken Boyer was intentionally walked, Rip Repulski drove a shot down the third-base line that the Braves' Eddie Mathews attempted to field. "All I was trying to do was get in front of it to block it," Mathews explained. "I didn't know where the hell the bounce was going to come. It hit me in the knee and bounced into foul territory and over to the stands."

When the ball caromed off Mathews's knee, Stan Musial scored the winning run. It was a devastating 2–1 loss for the Braves. As Spahn headed to the dugout, tears flowed freely down his cheeks. "Beyond a doubt, that Saturday game in St. Louis was the most heartbreaking moment I had in twenty-one years of baseball," Spahn remembered. "We had every reason to win, but it was like it wasn't meant to be."

Even Henry Aaron's league-leading .328 batting average couldn't save the team's evaporating pennant hopes. "We might as well have left our bats in the clubhouse," he said in his 1974 autobiography. "To this day, I believe we should have won the pennant that year, but we choked."

As expected, the entire Braves organization took the loss hard. "After the game, Quinn and I went to the top of the Chase Hotel for a drink," publicity director Donald Davidson remembered. "John looked out the window and said to me, 'Do you want to jump first, or do you want me to push you?'"

For the Braves' 1956 season finale, Burdette beat the Cardinals 4–2, but it was too late. Brooklyn had already completed the series sweep of Pittsburgh to repeat as National League champions. "We led the league 126 days. The Dodgers led the league only 17 days, but they led the last day and that was the right day," Aaron observed. "Man, you talk about something hurting. For the first time in my life in the big leagues, I really knew what hurt was."

As the players quietly dressed, Fred Haney entered the clubhouse. With their 92–62 record falling one game short of the pennant—their third second-place finish in four years—Milwaukee was again without an elusive World Series appearance. Instead of receiving a courtesy thank you and congrats, the players received a reception of cold conviction. "Boys," Haney told them. "Go home and have yourselves a nice winter. Relax. Have fun. Get good and rested, because when you get to Bradenton next year, you're going to have one helluva spring."

THE Pinnacle
1957-1958

"I don't think I ever saw a team open a season as determined to win as we did in 1957."
—HENRY AARON

The Braves of Bushville featured an eclectic roster, including the future all-time home-run king, a future NBA champion, six future big-league managers, and four future Hall of Famers. (ROBERT KOEHLER COLLECTION)

When Fred Haney called a team meeting before the first day of 1957 spring training, the Braves quickly realized the season would be vastly different from years past. Accustomed to "Jolly Cholly" Grimm's easygoing managerial style, the players gathered around expecting to hear an energetic pep talk. Instead, the Braves' manager made good on his promise from the previous September of giving them "one helluva spring." For six weeks Haney put the players through hours of practice and extensive conditioning, often followed by intrasquad games. He left no room for excuses or exceptions during his militant workouts. "We were there to practice being perfect, and the less perfect we were the better shape we got into," Henry Aaron recalled in his autobiography *Aaron*. Whenever an error was made, during either practice or intrasquad games, the entire team dropped what they were doing and ran a lap around the ballpark. "By the time we broke camp," Aaron said, "I swear that I knew every blade of grass around that fence by its first name."

Milwaukee was considered the odds-on favorite to win the 1957 National League pennant, and Haney refused to watch the Braves endure another pennant-race collapse. "With the experience of last year," Haney told reporters during spring training, "with the entire nation pulling for us and the wonderful reaction of the Milwaukee fans who met us at the airport on our return from St. Louis after losing, I think it would take a man with a heart of stone not to have the determination to bring a winner to these wonderful people."

By the time Fred Haney's Braves broke camp in Bradenton, they were slim, trim, and hungry to vindicate themselves after the previous season's disappointing finish. "I don't think I ever saw a team open a season as determined to win as we did in 1957," Aaron said.

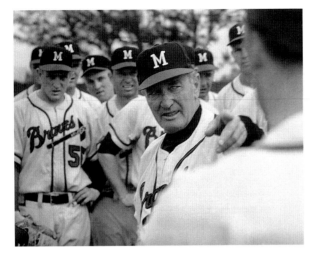

Braves manager Fred Haney (pointing) was called "Little Napoleon" by many of his players due to his 5'6" stature and strict workout regimens. (WHI IMAGE ID 49246)

> ## "Lou would make coffee nervous."
> –FRED HANEY

Fred Haney (2) with his Braves coaching staff (from left to right) Charlie Root, Connie Ryan, John Riddle, and Robert Keely (ROBERT KOEHLER COLLECTION)

Thirty-six-year-old Warren Spahn took the mound for the Braves in the opener at Chicago's Wrigley Field. Fully recovered from several off-season cartilage operations on his knees, Spahn continued to dominate National League batsmen. The Braves ace retired the last fourteen men he faced en route to a four-hit, 4–1 Opening Day win. "I think he can pitch a couple more years, anyhow. He doesn't have the blazing stuff anymore, but his knowledge of the hitters is a big help to him," Haney admitted to reporters. "Spahnie goes on like ol' man river because he works hard to keep in shape."

The Braves started the 1957 season uncharacteristically fast, winning their first five games. The streak included their fifth consecutive home opener victory at County Stadium as Lou Burdette hurled a six-hit shutout against Cincinnati. Burdette's gestures, mound antics, and delivery often suggested he was throwing an illegal spitball. "The way I described it is he threw a 'dry spitter,'" Del Crandall explained. "His ball just moved down a lot. He had a great sinker. Some hitters were always complaining. It was laughable. Lou just threw sinkers, sliders and screwballs."

With his fidgeting mannerisms, Burdette inspired Fred Haney to suggest that "Lou would make coffee nervous." Opposing teams often scrutinized the right-hander as he went through countless gyrations between pitches, leading hitters to believe the ball was wet—even if it wasn't. "I don't believe Burdette ever had an interview when he wasn't asked if he threw a spitball," Donald Davidson said. "He had a standard answer: 'I don't know how you guys can ask me a silly question like that. They always accuse me of throwing it. I never did even though I've been told by hitters that certain pitches I threw did funny things on the way to the plate. Having the batters think I was throwing spitters gave me a psychological advantage.'"

Nobody was more accusatory of Burdette's supposed cheating than Redlegs' manager Birdie Tebbetts. The

Lou Burdette was known for quick gestures to his cap, mouth, and forehead that deceived many paranoid hitters—and helped him post a 17–9 record with a 3.72 ERA in 1957. (DAVID KLUG COLLECTION)

Cincinnati skipper was so determined to catch Burdette in the act of doctoring the ball that on April 27 he had slow-motion cameras placed around Cincinnati's Crosley Field. Unable to gather any substantial proof, Tebbetts and the Redlegs were forced to watch Burdette beat them 5–4 behind homers from Henry Aaron and Joe Adcock.

During those first ten games of the season, the Braves built an early three-game lead almost solely on the arms of Spahn and Burdette. Managing the schedule to take advantage of open dates, Haney kept his two aces on the mound, while Bob Buhl, Ernie Johnson, Red Murff, and Dave Jolly saw minimal action during the first few weeks of the season. "I worked my men in spring training with that in mind," Haney told the press. "I worked the others, too—in batting practice, running them in the outfield. And I explained my intentions to them. You've got to be honest to gain confidence."

But Haney's strategy soon sputtered as the Braves fell into a malaise. After Cincinnati won nine games in a row to catapult past Milwaukee in the standings, Haney called out his entire team during a closed-door meeting in May and told them, "You're playing like you played last September."

By mid-June the Braves had slid down to fourth place in a five-team pennant race, with only two and a half games separating the front-running Redlegs from the fifth-place Cardinals. With tension rising in the Milwaukee clubhouse, the team needed a spark. Tempers finally boiled over in Brooklyn on June 13, when Billy Bruton's second

Milwaukee Braves "bonus babies" Hawk Taylor (19), Mel Roach (29), Joey Jay (42), and John DeMerit (18) signed in an era when there was a wide-open market for amateur players. In an attempt to keep signing bonuses under control, players who received more than a $6,000 reward for turning pro were prohibited from being sent to the minor leagues for two years. The flawed system often prevented players from maturing in the minors and eventually led to the birth of the amateur draft. (ROBERT KOEHLER COLLECTION)

home run of the day led to the Dodgers' Don Drysdale flagrantly planting a fastball in Johnny Logan's ribs. As the Braves' feisty shortstop trotted to first base, he glared at the Dodgers hurler from under his bushy black eyebrows. "Try coming into second base some time," he yelled, adding a few choice phrases regarding Drysdale's ancestry.

"Why wait?" Drysdale defiantly replied. "Let's do it now."

Never one to back down from a fight, Logan charged the mound. Eddie Mathews, who had been watching from the on-deck circle, raced onto the field to back up his teammate. "Eddie did not start many fights, but he finished several," Donald Davidson reminisced. "Mathews rescued Logan so often that they called him John's relief fighter."

The Braves' fearless third baseman knocked down Brooklyn's towering rookie pitcher with one wicked right hook. Not until Brooklyn's Gil Hodges dragged Mathews away by his ankles did the pummeling of Drysdale cease. The fight seemed to ignite the Braves, and a Carl Sawatski home run helped Milwaukee beat Brooklyn to put them atop the National League standings for the first time in nearly a month.

With the midseason trading deadline about to expire on June 15, general manager John Quinn still sought the magic formula that would stabilize the inconsistent Braves. He decided the team was in need of some veteran leadership with postseason experience. As the midnight trade deadline approached, Quinn finalized a deal

Johnny Logan (23) hurled punches at any Dodgers that got in his way during a June 13, 1957, brawl. (COURTESY OF MIKE RODELL)

Braves owner Lou Perini and general manager John Quinn (WHI IMAGE ID 49051)

that sent frontline players Bobby Thomson, Ray Crone, and Danny O'Connell to the Giants for second baseman Red Schoendienst. "When we traded for Red, that solidified our infield. He knew talent and would position different fielders accordingly. He was like a manager on the field," Braves' veteran outfielder Andy Pafko recalled. Arriving with a reputation as a smooth fielder and tough hitter from either side of the plate, Schoendienst immediately took O'Connell's place on the roster. Looking to fill the holes left by the departed Thomson and Crone, Milwaukee called up power-hitting Wes Covington to platoon in left field and twenty-seven-year-old hurler Don McMahon to provide some much-needed late-inning relief.

Then on June 23 at County Stadium, Joe Adcock broke his right leg while sliding into second base, sidelining him until September. "I'm surprised that Joe hadn't broken something before when he slid," Aaron recalled. "He was a lot of a man, and when he hit the dirt it was like a horse sliding. You could almost feel the ground shake."

In need of an immediate replacement, the Braves turned to Brooklyn native Frank Torre. Known more for his glove than his bat, he did little to boost hopes that Milwaukee would capture the pennant in 1957. "We were in second place," Torre remembered, "and all the media sort of kissed us good-bye."

Reserves Frank Torre and Nippy Jones played vital roles in the Braves' quest for the 1957 National League pennant. (ROBERT KOEHLER COLLECTION)

Right before the All-Star break, the Braves continued to slump, losing five of seven games and dropping two and a half games behind the first-place Cardinals. Once again, Milwaukee was well represented during the Midsummer Classic at St. Louis's Sportsman's Park, with Henry Aaron, Lou Burdette, Johnny Logan, Eddie Mathews, Red Schoendienst, and Warren Spahn selected to the All-Star squad. Despite their efforts, the National League lost 6–5.

The pennant race reconvened with the Cardinals, Braves, Dodgers, Redlegs, and Phillies desperately trying to put together a winning streak. With the slightest injury or lapse in judgment forfeiting a team's chances, the Braves thought they watched their pennant hopes literally crash onto the outfield grass on July 11, when Billy Bruton collided with short-

> "I don't know what happens to suddenly make a minor league ballplayer into Babe Ruth, but Hazle was right out of 'The Twilight Zone.'"
>
> —EDDIE MATHEWS

stop Felix Mantilla while chasing a pop fly into short center field. "I was goin' at full speed and Bruton was comin' at full speed," Mantilla recounted. "We collided, and I went like fifteen feet up in the air and Bruton went the other way. It was ugly." Both players got up with a little help, but the damage was done. Mantilla's injury kept him out of nineteen games. Bruton's torn right knee ligaments left him on the disabled list for the remainder of the season. Two days later, outfield replacement Andy Pafko got hurt while making a sliding catch. "All of a sudden Del Crandall had to take off his mask and chest protector and become a right fielder," Braves historian Bob Buege explained. "Even recently acquired second baseman Red Schoendienst and first baseman Nippy Jones had to take their turns as fly-catchers."

Desperate for outfield assistance, the Braves were about to call up Earl Hersh from their Wichita farm club. Instead, Wichita manager Ben Geraghty lobbied for Bob Hazle and his hot bat to be given a chance. After being acquired by Milwaukee the previous season in a trade with the Cincinnati Redlegs for George Crowe, Hazle had almost quit baseball but decided to play one more season. He started the 1957 season at Wichita and was hitting just .220 when he suddenly caught fire and Geraghty recommended him to be called up. Nicknamed after a storm that hit the South Carolina coast in 1954, Bob "Hurricane" Hazle was supposed to ride the Braves' bench as outfield insurance but soon found himself storming through National League pitching rotations. "I don't know what happens to suddenly make a minor league ballplayer into Babe Ruth," Eddie Mathews confessed, "but Hazle was right out of 'The Twilight Zone.' We were hanging in there pretty well before he arrived, but he just picked us up."

Beginning on July 31, the Braves went on to win the first nine games Hazle started, and by August 6 the team had regained first place. Before anyone could stop the Braves in mid-August, they had won ten games in a row, all by lopsided scores. Even the Dodgers couldn't slow them down. On August 24 the Braves tore through eight Brooklyn pitchers during a 13–7 thrashing, tying the National League record for most hurlers used in one game. The following day, Bob Hazle, who had been hitting a blazing .526 since being called up, hit two two-run homers as Warren Spahn beat the Phillies.

Milwaukee's firepower continued to devour opposing pitching staffs. On September 2 the Braves whipped the Cubs at Wrigley Field in a doubleheader sweep. Bob Hazle showed no signs of slowing down after going four-for-seven in the first game, with three doubles and two RBIs in Milwaukee's 23–10 pummeling. "He was hotter than a firecracker. Every time he swung the bat, it seemed like he got a base hit," Red Schoendienst remembered. Frank Torre, still subbing at first base for the injured Adcock, tied a major-league record by scoring six of the Braves' twenty-three runs. In the second game Bob Trowbridge hurled a masterful three-hitter as Milwaukee

Hitting .403 in 134 at bats in 1957, Bob "Hurricane" Hazle joined Ted Williams, who hit .406 in 1941, as the only two players to hit .400 in at least 150 plate appearances since 1930. (ROBERT KOEHLER COLLECTION)

handcuffed the Cubs' bats in a 4–0 shutout. The following day Spahn whitewashed Chicago, 8–0, for his forty-first career shutout, setting a career record for left-handed pitchers.

The Braves finally cooled after Labor Day, but not before winning seventeen of nineteen and twenty-four of twenty-nine games to build an eight-and-a-half-game lead. By losing eight of eleven in a September slump, the Braves allowed St. Louis to shave six games off their lead. "We lost enough ballgames in September to keep it interesting," Mathews admitted.

On September 15, following their third straight loss, the Braves' lead was down to just two and a half games. "Terrible nightmares of 1956's final weekend collapse began to recur among the Milwaukee faithful," Bob Buege observed.

Following the loss, Haney kept the clubhouse door closed for an hour. When he finally opened it, reporters and photographers burst into the room. Haney turned to his players and reminded them of just what would happen if the team continued to slide. "Here are your pallbearers, gentlemen. Don't you want to meet your pallbearers?"

Following the meeting, the team won five straight behind a revived pitching staff. Bob Buhl, Bob Trowbridge, and Lou Burdette won complete games, and Warren Spahn won his twentieth game of the season, followed by Buhl's second victory within five days.

RIGHT: Eddie Mathews's fielding and cannon arm at third base (above) continued to improve as he led the league in assists, while across the diamond first baseman Frank Torre (below) led all National League first basemen in fielding percentage in 1957. (ROBERT KOEHLER COLLECTION)

With six games remaining, the Braves had a five-game lead over the second-place Cardinals. Arriving in Milwaukee for a three-game series, St. Louis was looking to keep its pennant hopes alive with a series sweep. "After what happened in 1956, we were taking nothing for granted. We had shown that we were capable of choking, and deep down everybody was afraid it might happen again," Aaron confessed.

An anxious crowd of 40,926 fans filed into County Stadium for the series' first game on September 23. Milwaukee jumped off to a quick 1–0 lead in the second inning, while Burdette kept St. Louis off the scoreboard for the first five innings. After yielding a pair of runs in the top of the sixth, the Braves tied the game at two in the bottom of the seventh. With the game still tied after nine innings, Milwaukee appeared poised to win in the tenth inning after loading the bases with one out—until pinch hitter Frank Torre bounced into a rally-killing double play. "The crowd was so deflated at that point," recalled future baseball commissioner Bud Selig, who was in the County Stadium stands that night.

After Red Schoendienst made the first out in the home half of the eleventh inning, Johnny Logan kept the Braves' pennant hopes alive with a single to center. When

By 1957 the Braves Booster Club was the largest in baseball, with more than thirty thousand estimated members. (MILWAUKEE JOURNAL SENTINEL)

Eddie Mathews proceeded to fly out, the crowd grew even more anxious. "Everybody was shouting and throwing something, and County Stadium was losing its mind," Henry Aaron recalled. "But I remember looking up about halfway down the first base line and noticing the time on the big clock hanging above the fence. It was 11:34."

Aaron stepped into the batter's box to face Billy Muffett, who was fresh from the Cardinals' minor-league affiliate in Houston. On his first pitch, Muffett threw a slow curve hoping Aaron was expecting a fastball. Aaron's quick wrists adjusted, and he connected on the pitch—a towering hit toward the center-field fence. At the 402-foot sign, St. Louis

When Braves second base-
man Red Schoendienst (4)
tried to field pitcher Bob
Buhl's pickoff toss in Game
Three, the ball went into
center field, and the Yankees' Mickey Mantle (7)
raced to third on the error.
(DAVID KLUG COLLECTION)

five Milwaukee hits in seven and one-third innings of relief. Meanwhile, New York's rookie shortstop Tony Kubek almost single-handedly outhit the Braves' entire lineup. By knocking in four runs with three hits, including two homers, Kubek and the Yankees assaulted Milwaukee's bullpen en route to a 12–3 thrashing. "It sobered the Milwaukee fans some," Henry Aaron conceded. "Worst thing about it is, we're in our own ballpark, but the Yankees have taken us apart, humiliated us before our own people in the only game we've played there."

With the demoralizing loss, the Braves were under tremendous pressure to rebound. In front of another capacity County Stadium crowd for Game Four, Warren Spahn tossed a steady stream of groundouts for eight innings. Meanwhile, the Braves built a comfortable 4–1 lead behind an Aaron three-run homer and a Frank Torre solo shot. In the top of the ninth, the Braves were within one out of evening the Series at two when Spahn unraveled. Having given up eleventh-hour hits to Yogi Berra and Gil McDougald, Spahn held a 3–2 count on New York's Elston Howard—and surrendered the game-tying home run into the left-field stands. A tomblike silence fell over County Stadium. "We could have folded then. I really believe that," Aaron recalled. "You never saw a quieter dugout in your life when we came in from the field. We all looked as if we'd been watching a murder."

The Yankees shut down the Braves bats in the bottom of the ninth. In the top of the tenth, outfielder Hank Bauer tripled to drive home Kubek. New York was only three outs away from a 5–4 victory, and Braves manager Fred Haney was facing another demoralizing defeat. To lead off the home half of the inning, Haney opted for

For over an hour before the start of Game Four, traffic clogged all three westbound lanes across the Wisconsin Avenue viaduct as fans filed into the County Stadium parking lot. (MILWAUKEE JOURNAL SENTINEL)

reserve infielder Vernal "Nippy" Jones to pinch-hit for Spahn. "I don't think there's any doubt about what was the turning point in the 1957 World Series," Aaron declared.

Although Jones had not played in the big leagues since 1952, the Braves had purchased his contract from Sacramento of the Pacific Coast League in July as first-base insurance. He was used sparingly during the 1957 season, appearing in just thirty regular-season games. But Nippy Jones's first World Series appearance in a Milwaukee uniform would not be forgotten. Jones's first pitch from Yankees reliever Tommy Byrne went wild. "The ball hit me on the foot and I dropped my bat and started toward first base," Jones recounted. "But [umpire] Augie Donatelli said, 'Come back here. That's ball one.' I couldn't believe it."

The County Stadium crowd of 45,804 couldn't quite decipher the ruckus at home plate as Jones questioned the call. "Jones wasn't the talkative sort. But he was talking now, and he was having it out with Donatelli chin to chin," Aaron remembered.

As Jones argued his case, the ball rolled back toward the plate after hitting the concrete backstop. "I went right for the ball," Jones admitted, "and Yogi Berra was pretty smart, so he did the same thing. I got there first, and there was a spot of shoe polish about a half-inch in diameter [on the ball]."

When Donatelli saw the scuff mark, he awarded Jones first base. "Nippy was very meticulous about his uniform and how it looked, including his shoes. He insisted that the clubhouse boys polish his shoes before every game," Eddie Mathews remembered. "Good thing he did. If that ball had hit my shoe, you wouldn't have known it."

A Braves reception committee including Wes Covington (43), Eddie Mathews (41), and Johnny Logan (upper right) welcomed Henry Aaron (44) home after his three-run homer in the fourth inning gave Milwaukee an early lead. (DAVID KLUG COLLECTION)

Nippy Jones (25) was awarded first base after umpire Augie Donatelli showed Yankees catcher Yogi Berra (8) the shoe polish scuff mark on the ball. (DAVID KLUG COLLECTION)

Sensing a rally, Haney pulled Jones in favor of pinch runner Felix Mantilla. Red Schoendienst proceeded to sacrifice bunt Mantilla to second, allowing scrappy shortstop Johnny Logan to bat with the tying run in scoring position. Playing on an injured ankle that had to be drained before the game, Logan stepped to the plate with hopes of putting the ball into play: "All I could think of was base hit, base hit, base hit. I kept telling myself not to go for the long ball." After waiting on the first two pitches, Logan slammed a clutch line drive into left field, bringing in Mantilla to tie the game at five. As the ball bounced into the left-field corner, the Braves shortstop entertained thoughts of heading toward third, "so Eddie could drive me in with a long fly, but I couldn't take the gamble."

Logan's discretion left him at second when Mathews, who was 1-for-11 with the bat for the Series, stepped to the plate with one on and one out. "Before the game I had been thinking about Gil Hodges going 0-for-21 in the 1952 World Series," Mathews confessed. "A Milwaukee sportswriter handed me three pennies and said, 'Put these in your pocket for good luck.' I wasn't the slightest bit superstitious, but what the hell, I put them in my uniform pocket. I wasn't hitting worth two cents, so maybe three would help." Taking the count to 2–2, Mathews swung at a hip-high fastball. "I was worried for a second when I saw Hank Bauer in front of the right field fence, pounding his glove like he was going to make the catch," he said. "I didn't see the ball go into the seats, but the crowd reaction left no doubt that it was a home run."

Eddie Mathews (41) was greeted at home plate after his tenth-inning home run evened the Series at two games apiece. (DAVID KLUG COLLECTION)

The towering two-run blast broke Mathews's slump and rejuvenated the entire Braves squad. "Ball game, 7–5, from death to life again." Aaron exclaimed. "We knew we could win then, but not if it hadn't been for Nippy Jones."

When Nippy Jones returned to the dugout earlier in the inning, his box score statistics for Game Four consisted of a series of consecutive zeros—uncharacteristic stats for a World Series hero who had just made his last major-league appearance. "The importance of the event seemed to grow as time went on. The main thing to me was winning, and I didn't care how we did it," Jones remembered.

After Game Four Nippy Jones showed Braves equipment manager Joe Taylor the scuff mark left on the baseball from his polished shoes. (DAVID KLUG COLLECTION)

Game Five found the Yankees helpless against Burdette's wicked sinker, as Whitey Ford simultaneously handcuffed the Braves' bats. Both pitchers kept the game scoreless for five full innings, with Burdette's shutout preserved by Wes Covington, whose wall-jumping, fence-crashing grab in the fourth inning kept a potential Gil McDougald home run out of the County Stadium stands. As the dueling aces battled into the sixth, Ford was almost out of the inning when Eddie Mathews stepped into the batter's box. In what should have been the third out of the inning, Mathews bounced a high chopper toward the right side of the infield. Yankees second baseman Jerry Coleman fielded the ball cleanly but misjudged Mathews's speed, and the Braves' third baseman was safe at first. Aaron followed with a pop-up into short right, and Hank Bauer sprinted in as Coleman raced out to field the ball. As it dropped between them for a single, Mathews sped to third. Adcock slashed a single to bring Mathews home, giving the Braves a 1–0 lead. It was all Burdette needed, as he scattered just three more hits in the final three innings for a complete-game shutout. "When Lou needed to make a pitch, he did it," Del Crandall said. "They didn't hit many balls good off him. He was in and out, up and down . . . a little of this and a little of that. He just made great pitches. The Yankees couldn't get comfortable looking for anything because he had everything working with just enough movement to keep it off the center of their bats. His location was outstanding." With the 1–0 victory, Milwaukee held a three-games-to-two advantage as the World Series returned to New York.

The Yankees returned home to the "House That Ruth Built" with no intention of folding in Game Six. Once again, New York pounced on Braves starter Bob Buhl, and he failed to make it out of the third inning. Facing a two-run deficit, the Braves' starting first baseman Frank Torre stepped to the plate to lead off the fifth inning. Playing in Yankee Stadium was something of a homecoming for the Brooklyn native. With dozens of his family and friends among the 61,408 fans in the stands, Torre cranked a home run off Yankees starter Bob Turley to cut New York's lead in half. "I don't even remember running around the bases," Torre said. "It was a tremendous thrill, especially with my mother and one of my sisters at the game."

In the top of the seventh, Aaron clobbered a solo homer to tie the game at two. Then, in the bottom half of the inning, the Yankees got to reliever Ernie Johnson as Hank Bauer connected for a solo home run off the left-field foul pole. Trailing 3–2, the Braves began a rally in the ninth, but after Mathews walked, Covington grounded into the game-ending double play, forcing the deciding Game Seven. After six weeks of spring training, 154 regular-season games, and six World Series contests, baseball's 1957 world champion wouldn't be decided until the season's last possible day.

> **"When Lou needed to make a pitch, he did it."**
> **–DEL CRANDALL**

BELOW, LEFT: Wes Covington hung onto the ball after his leaping catch in left field near the 355-foot sign nabbed a long blow from Gil McDougald in the fourth inning of Game Five. (DAVID KLUG COLLECTION)

BELOW, RIGHT: During Game Five Lou Burdette threw only eighty-seven pitches against the Yankees and allowed just two fly balls to the outfield. (DAVID KLUG COLLECTION)

ABOVE, LEFT: Braves catcher Del Rice tagged out the Yankees' Yogi Berra at home plate on a throw from left fielder Wes Covington at the top of the ninth. (DAVID KLUG COLLECTION)

ABOVE, RIGHT: Fred Haney (left), Del Rice (7), Taylor Phillips (in jacket), and other ecstatic players greeted catcher Del Crandall (1) after his eighth-inning home run gave Milwaukee a commanding 5–0 lead in the Series-deciding seventh game. (DAVID KLUG COLLECTION)

ABOVE: In 1957 the New York Yankees had been shut out only twice during their entire 154-game regular season. But Lou Burdette shut them out twice within four days and beat them three times to earn the World Series' Most Valuable Player award. (DAVID KLUG COLLECTION)

RIGHT: The victorious Braves hugged one another on the mound. Later they would cash World Series checks of $8,924.36 each. (NATIONAL BASEBALL HALL OF FAME LIBRARY)

Conley gave up a run, and the Braves lost 4–3, their first home opener loss since moving to Milwaukee. The team quickly made amends, winning their next three contests behind fine pitching performances from Burdette and Buhl and a shutout by Spahn. Milwaukee's typical slow start left them with a respectable 8–5 record and a half game behind the first-place Giants by the end of April.

As reigning kings of the National League, Fred Haney's crew was tested early and often. The Braves' manager was forced to juggle lineups due to nagging injuries and disappointing performances. "All year the outfield was a matter of 'Who can play today?' One day Haney had seven infielders in the starting lineup, with Adcock, Mantilla and Harry Hanebrink playing outfield," third baseman Eddie Mathews explained.

Still mending from his collision with Felix Mantilla the previous season, Billy Bruton didn't begin patrolling center field until May 24. Wes Covington's knee injury during spring training would limit him to just 90 games over the course of the 154-game regular season. The Braves' surprise spark of '57, Bob "Hurricane" Hazle, was sold to Detroit after starting the 1958 season hitting a frigid .179. According to Eddie Mathews, "The other ballplayers were completely stunned and upset about it. Here was a guy who came out of nowhere and led us, not single-handedly, but led us to our first World Series. He was in a slump for the first month of 1958, but he'd had some ankle trouble in spring. We figured the ball club owed him more than that."

Bob Buhl's numerous arm ailments sidelined him in May after he started the season hot with three straight victories. Second baseman Red Schoendienst was limited to just 106 games as he suffered through bruised ribs, a broken finger, and pleurisy in 1958. But it was a series of inexplicable symptoms that truly affected his play. "I wasn't feeling that good. I was really run down. I knew something was wrong, and I knew it wasn't just a cold," Schoendienst remembered.

The injuries had crippled the Braves potent lineup and dependable pitching staff; nevertheless, the Braves spent most of the season's first half bobbing in and out of first place. Although Milwaukee stood atop the National League standings alongside the Giants, who had found early-season success in their new San Francisco surroundings, manager Fred Haney felt his talented team should have been dominating the competition.

When the Braves arrived in California for their inaugural West Coast road trip, Haney harped on his squad for being too comfortable and lacking focus. "It's a funny thing," the Braves' skipper surmised, "but a manager can't get a player to listen to him the way another player can. Coming from a manager, it's critical. Coming from a player, it's constructive."

Desperate to motivate his players, Haney began to invite his celebrity friends from his days as manager of the Hollywood Stars minor-league team into the clubhouse.

Manager Fred Haney was hung in effigy after the Braves lost their fifth straight game on July 5, 1958. (MILWAUKEE JOURNAL SENTINEL)

"Fred was Mr. Hollywood," Eddie Mathews said. "He knew everybody out there. He liked to bring in movie stars to talk to us, I guess to impress us. One time he brought Pat O'Brien into the clubhouse to give us the Gipper speech from *The Knute Rockne Story*."

But the Braves couldn't seem to pull away from the pack in what became one of the tightest pennant races in recent years, with no team trailing first place by more than nine and a half games in June. Although they held a one-and-a-half-game lead over the Giants, the Braves had dropped eleven of twenty games during a three-week home stand. Milwaukeeans accustomed to winning were becoming disenchanted. On July 5 several hostile fans hung an effigy of manager Fred Haney from a construction crane at a downtown Milwaukee demolition site. "I think in 1957 the country wanted us to win the pennant and beat the Yankees. In 1958 I think they expected it." Mathews said.

Escaping the growing resentment in Milwaukee, Haney and the Braves' All-Star representatives—Henry Aaron, Del Crandall, Johnny Logan, Eddie Mathews, Don McMahon, and Warren Spahn—gathered in Baltimore on July 8 for the 1958 All-Star Game. The American League won 4–3 in a game that didn't feature an extra-base hit by either club.

Milwaukee ended its five-game losing streak on July 6 by shutting out the Pittsburgh Pirates 2–0 behind the pitching of Joey Jay (left) and Wes Covington (right), who homered in the seventh inning. (DAVID KLUG COLLECTION)

After the All-Star break, the Braves continued to fail in their attempts to extend their first-place lead. They dropped their West Coast opener in Los Angeles and struggled in San Francisco. After salvaging a sweep of the Cardinals in St. Louis and taking two of three from the Cubs in Chicago, the Braves returned to County Stadium on July 30 to begin a nineteen-game home stand.

With the opportunity to take sole possession of first place, Milwaukee sent Warren Spahn to the mound to face Los Angeles' Sandy Koufax. Seeking his first victory over the Dodgers in seven years, Spahn stayed on even terms with Koufax for seven innings. In Milwaukee's half of the eighth, with the game tied at three, Koufax served up Eddie Mathews's twenty-first home run of the season to secure the Braves' 4–3 victory. Spahn's jinx had been lifted as he beat the Dodgers for the first time since September 25, 1951.

The Braves entered August with a slim one-and-a-half-game lead over San Francisco, who arrived at County Stadium on August 1 for a crucial four-game series. Milwaukee polished them off in a four-game sweep en route to winning seventeen of twenty-two games. "The one thing that really held us up during the 1958 season was the pitching," Henry Aaron recalled.

Without the services of star hurlers Bob Buhl and Gene Conley due to arm ailments, Carlton Willey, Joey Jay, Juan Pizarro, and Bob Rush performed magnificently for the Braves all year. Led by Spahn and Burdette, the club's revamped pitching corps all but vanquished the rest of the National League during the second half of the season. During a crucial mid-August series in Philadelphia, Braves pitchers smothered the Phillies in a four-game sweep. Willey threw a shutout in the first game, 1–0. Spahn took the second game 2–1, followed by Juan Pizarro and Lou Burdette winning both ends of a doubleheader, 5–1 and 4–1. During the month of August, Spahn had won four games, Willey five, and Burdette seven as Milwaukee extended its first-place lead to eight games over

> "I think in 1957 the country wanted us to win the pennant and beat the Yankees. In 1958 I think they expected it."
> —EDDIE MATHEWS

Carlton Willey hurled a shutout in his first big-league start, finished the season with a 2.70 ERA, and was selected by the Sporting News as its 1958 National League Rookie of the Year. (DAVID KLUG COLLECTION)

the fading Pirates and Giants. Nobody appreciated the young hurlers' efforts more than manager Fred Haney. "They sure came through for me," he told reporters. "Barring injuries, they should be winning for a long time."

On September 21 in Cincinnati, with the chance to clinch their second consecutive National League pennant hanging in the balance, the Braves turned to Warren Spahn. With a four-run fifth inning followed by a two-run homer from Aaron in the seventh, Milwaukee slugged its way to a 6–5 win, giving Spahn his twenty-first victory of the year. The Braves had secured their second consecutive National League pennant and held an impromptu celebration in the clubhouse after the game. "We won the pennant by eight games that year—the same margin we won by in 1957—but somehow there wasn't quite the atmosphere that we'd enjoyed the season before," Aaron recalled. "Maybe it was just that we expected the same magic all over again and that was impossible, because 1957 was a once-in-a-lifetime experience."

The Braves won four of their final six games to finish with a 92–62 record, winning the pennant with three fewer victories than the prior season. While many teams had suffered drops in attendance following world championship seasons, Milwaukee had always run contrary to conventional baseball attendance trends. But after pulling in a record 2.2 million in 1957, Milwaukee County Stadium recorded only 1.97 million fans through its turnstiles in 1958. This slight but unmistakable decrease in attendance left Eddie Mathews to conclude, "Declining attendance said the Braves' product had lost some of its zest."

Also suffering a surprising drop in attendance were the Yankees, who with the departure of the Dodgers and Giants had become New York's sole baseball occupants in 1958. Winning ninety-two games and outdistancing the second-place White Sox by ten games, the Yankees were ready for their rematch with the Braves. "The Yankees didn't have much trouble getting to the World Series again, either. The two of us were far and away the class of our leagues, and we knew that if we could beat them twice in a row we would clearly establish ourselves as the best team in baseball," Aaron said.

Because the Braves were returning to the World Series as the reigning champs, they were no longer perceived as underdogs. "Whatever you do, don't get overconfident," Haney warned his players. "Maybe it looked easy, but it wasn't. And don't forget, we've still got a World Series to play."

◆　◆　◆

The 1958 World Series opened in Milwaukee with County Stadium filled to the rafters. Game One on October 1 featured the rematch of mound masters Whitey Ford and Warren Spahn. The Yankees grabbed an early lead on a Moose Skowron homer. The Braves battled back in the bottom half of the inning with a string of three singles

Eddie Mathews took deliberate aim in bunting during a pre-World Series practice. (DAVID KLUG COLLECTION)

> "Most of us were thinking that the World Series was over and that we were the greatest baseball team known to man."
>
> —HENRY AARON

by Crandall, Pafko, and Spahn. The Braves went ahead 2–1, but the lead lasted only into the top of the next inning. After Spahn walked Ford, Hank Bauer crushed a hanging screwball into the bleachers for a 3–2 New York lead.

Milwaukee tied it up in the home half of the eighth. Meanwhile, Spahn kept the Yankees bats quiet, scattering just seven hits through nine innings. In the decisive tenth inning, the Braves strung together three singles by Adcock, Crandall, and Bruton, who drove in Adcock with the winning run. With the 4–3 victory, Milwaukee captured the early 1–0 Series lead. "If you can win that first Series game, you're really floating along on clouds," Spahn asserted. "Your confidence in yourself and your team gets a tremendous boost, especially when you figure it takes only .500 ball to win at that point."

For Game Two, 46,367 Milwaukee fans watched the Yankees load the bases in the top of the first inning. "Tension was thick in Game Two because Lou Burdette, boasting 24 straight scoreless innings, needed only six more zips to break Babe Ruth's World Series pitching mark," Donald Davidson said.

The Yankees scored an unearned run in the first inning, ending Burdette's bid to break Ruth's series record of twenty-nine and two-thirds shutout innings. As New York took an early 1–0 lead into the bottom half of the frame, the Braves initiated the greatest first-inning bombardment in Series history. Led off by a home run by Billy Bruton and bookended with a three-run blast by Burdette, Milwaukee erupted for seven runs. With the early lead, Burdette coasted behind Milwaukee's fifteen-hit attack for the 13–5 win. Having tomahawked the Yankees during both games at County Stadium, the Braves were only two victories away from once again devastating baseball's most dominating team. "When we caught the plane to New York that night, most of us were thinking that the World Series was over and that we were the greatest baseball team known to man," Aaron remembered.

The story for Game Three in New York was Yankees starter Don Larsen, who silenced the Braves bats. Milwaukee's Bob Rush kept pace for the first four innings but walked the bases full with two outs in the fifth. As the Yankee Stadium crowd roared in the background, Bronx Bomber Hank Bauer came through with a single that scored two. In the seventh, Braves' reliever Don McMahon was unable to contain Bauer's

Lou Burdette (33) was congratulated by Billy Bruton (38) after hitting a three-run home run to extend the Braves' early 7–1 first-inning lead in Game Two. (ROBERT KOEHLER COLLECTION)

hot postseason bat and surrendered a two-run home run to give the Yankees a commanding 4–0 lead. Although Yankees reliever Ryne Duren was a bit wild during the last two innings, Milwaukee became the victim of a six-hit shutout.

Game Four featured the Braves' Warren Spahn once again facing Whitey Ford. The game remained scoreless until New York started to unravel in the top of the sixth. Facing into a fierce sun, Yankees' left fielder Norm Siebern misplayed a simple pop-up off the bat of Red Schoendienst that went for a triple. When Tony Kubek erred on a Johnny Logan grounder, Schoendienst scampered home for the game's first run. In the seventh, Siebern suffered another unforgivable defensive lapse. After he got a late jump on a soft, sinking flare to shallow left field, the ball fell in front of him and Crandall scored the Braves' third run of the game. With the comfortable lead, Spahn became untouchable and even managed to halt Hank Bauer's seventeen-game World Series hitting streak. Throwing 112 pitches while surrendering only two hits in the 3–0 victory, Spahn

Center fielder Billy Bruton was the man of the hour after his single in the tenth inning of Game One won the game for the Braves. He went on to have a great 1958 Series, connecting for seven hits and a .412 batting average. (DAVID KLUG COLLECTION)

Helping to give Milwaukee a commanding three-games-to-one Series lead, Red Schoendienst (left) connected for a triple in the sixth inning of Game Four and scored the Braves' first run, while his fielding helped preserve Warren Spahn's (right) two-hit shutout. (DAVID KLUG COLLECTION)

gave the Braves what appeared to be an insurmountable three-games-to-one Series lead. "Now there was no question about it," Aaron recalled, "it was just a matter of time. We were the greatest and we all knew it, but we didn't go around talking about it. It might have been better if somebody had popped off a little about how great we were. Then somebody could have shut them up, and we would have all been reminded that humility is something that even great teams have—even teams as great as the Milwaukee Braves of 1958."

Just nine innings away from their second consecutive world championship, the Braves sent Yankee-slayer Lou Burdette to the mound for Game Five. After Gil McDougald homered in the third to give the Yankees an early 1–0 lead, the New York sun began casting some menacing shadows onto the Yankee Stadium diamond. "We found out the hard way that the Yankees, for example, are a team you've got to keep under your thumb every minute if you expect to beat them in a big game," Spahn remembered.

Looking to mount a rally in the top of the sixth, Billy Bruton led off with a single. Red Schoendienst followed with a liner into left with hopes of advancing the speedster. Yankees left fielder Elston Howard fought the glare and dove to his knees while sticking out his glove to make a circus catch. Caught off first, Bruton was doubled up. All of a sudden Milwaukee had nobody on and two outs. It may have been the turning point in the Series. The Yankees finally figured out Burdette in their half of the sixth and smashed their Series nemesis for six runs. Behind Bob Turley's powerful ten-strikeout, five-hit shutout, the Yankees pulled to within a game of tying the Series with the 7–0 victory.

Following the flogging, doubt began to plague the Braves players as they returned to Milwaukee for Games Six and Seven. "You could tell on the plane that we weren't quite sure we were as great as we had thought we were the day before," Aaron revealed.

Milwaukee hoped Warren Spahn could deliver the decisive knockout punch in Game Six at County Stadium. Although Haney's doubters felt the Braves manager was asking too much of his thirty-seven-year-old ace by pitching him on limited rest, Spahn had already won two games in the Series and was trying to win his third to duplicate Burdette's feat from the year before.

In the top of the first, New York's Hank Bauer powered his fourth Series home run into the left-field bleachers, but the Braves responded by touching up Yankees starter Whitey Ford to tie the score at one after one. Pitching on just two days' rest,

Ford was pulled in the second inning after the Braves took a 2–1 lead on singles by Covington, Pafko, and Spahn. When Schoendienst walked to load the bases, Art Ditmar took the hill for the Yankees to face Johnny Logan. The Braves' shortstop hit a short fly ball into left field. As Elston Howard made the catch, Pafko tagged up at third but was nailed at the plate with a rocket throw.

The Yankees tied the score in the sixth, and the game stayed deadlocked at 2 through regulation. In the top of the tenth, Gil McDougald connected for a home run off Spahn to break the tie. With two outs, Howard and Yogi Berra singled, prompting Haney to call for reliever Don McMahon. But he didn't quiet the Yankees bats, and

A headfirst slide by Andy Pafko (right) in the second inning of Game Six wasn't enough to avoid the tag from Yankees catcher Yogi Berra (left). (DAVID KLUG COLLECTION)

Automobiles filled the County Stadium parking lot before Game Seven of the 1958 Series. (MILWAUKEE JOURNAL SENTINEL)

Moose Skowron smacked a single to score a vital insurance run. In need of two runs, the Braves hitters were more than capable of making up the deficit.

Determined to finish the Series in six games, the Braves' Red Schoendienst led off the home half of the tenth inning with a grounder to second base. The usually sure-handed Gil McDougald fumbled the ball as the crowd roared in anticipation of a rally. But the second baseman quickly recovered and managed to throw Schoendienst out. Johnny Logan worked a walk off the Yankees' bespectacled smoke-ball artist Ryne Duren, keeping the Braves' hopes for a rally alive. After Eddie Mathews struck out, Aaron singled. Joe Adcock followed with another single that drove Logan home to narrow the gap to 4–3. But Bob Turley came on in relief for the Yankees and retired Frank Torre on a lineout to second base. With the ten-inning, 4–3 triumph, New York had tied the Series at three games apiece. But the Braves were still confident they could repeat as world champions. "We thought we could beat them before the first game, and we still thought we could beat them before the last one," Spahn insisted.

As Game Seven's 1:00 p.m. start time approached, the Milwaukee crowd of 46,367 shuffled into County Stadium with guarded optimism. Although Lou Burdette was pitching, they were all too aware that a loss would make the Braves the first club since the 1925 Washington Senators to lose the Series after being up three games to one.

After Burdette pitched a perfect top half of the first inning, the Braves looked to rout Yankees starter Don Larsen—just as they had done in the third inning of 1957's Game Seven. Red Schoendienst opened the bottom half with a single, followed by a Billy Bruton walk. Frank Torre then sacrificed the runners to second and third. Immediately going into ninth-inning strategy, Yankees' manager Casey Stengel ordered Aaron intentionally walked to load the bases. Wes Covington followed by grounding out to first, allowing Schoendienst to score the game's vital first run. As Bruton stood on third and Aaron at second, Stengel ordered Eddie Mathews intentionally walked. With the bases loaded and the opportunity to break the game wide open, Del Crandall stepped to the plate. But he took a called third strike. The Yankees had avoided disaster and now trailed by just one run.

To lead off the Yankees' second inning, Burdette walked Yogi Berra. Elston Howard followed with a sacrifice bunt toward first baseman Frank Torre. As Burdette ran to cover first, Torre's throw was behind him and bounced off his glove. With everybody safe, the Yankees had runners on first and third with no outs. Jerry Lumpe hit a grounder to Torre, who held Berra at third but again made a throw that Burdette couldn't handle. Charged with his second throwing error, Torre was frustrated. "I don't think I deserved the errors," he disclosed to reporters after the game, "but if you want to have a goat, it might as well be me."

With the bases loaded, Moose Skowron hit into a force play at second to score Berra. After Milwaukee native Tony Kubek drove in the Yankees' second run with a sacrifice fly, the Braves had also avoided a disaster. Despite the bad inning and a 2–1 deficit, the Braves seemed ready to take command in the third when Bruton led off with a single. After Larsen gave up another single to Aaron with one out, Casey Stengel made what many considered the key move of the game. Looking to extinguish another Braves rally, he called for hard-throwing right-hander Bob Turley. All Turley had done in the previous three days was pitch a five-hit shutout in the fifth game and get the final out in the Yankees' Game Six victory. With one out and two runners on base, Turley got Covington to ground out. Stengel once again ordered Mathews walked intentionally. For the second time in three innings, Del Crandall stepped to the plate with the bases loaded. Once again he couldn't capitalize and grounded out to second, ending the inning. In the sixth, Crandall redeemed himself with a solo home run to tie the game at two.

As the game went into the late innings, the tension at County Stadium continued to rise. For seven innings, Burdette and Turley had staged tremendous theater, with a plethora of ground balls and fast outs to keep the game close. In the eighth, Burdette

> **"I don't think I deserved the errors, but if you want to have a goat, it might as well be me."**
> —FRANK TORRE

Following his stellar 1957 World Series MVP performance, Lou Burdette finished the 1958 Series with a 1-2 record and 5.64 ERA. (ROBERT KOEHLER COLLECTION)

retired the first two Yankees batters. Then Berra hit a drive off the right-field wall for a double. Elston Howard followed by smacking a bouncer up the middle, just beyond the reach of shortstop Johnny Logan. The hit scored Berra and gave the Yankees a 3–2 lead. Pinch hitter Andy Carey followed with a single off the glove of third baseman Eddie Mathews that left runners on first and third. "The Yanks will play for one run at a time, but they can break open a ball game with a big inning at any time," Spahn declared.

Manager Fred Haney refused to go to his bullpen and allowed Burdette the opportunity to pitch out of the jam. Moose Skowron proceeded to crank Burdette's usually unhittable changeup into the left-center stands for a devastating three-run homer. With one swing of his bat, Skowron had psychologically crushed the County Stadium crowd. The Braves trailed 6–2 with just six outs left in the 1958 World Series. What had been a frenzied Game Seven a half inning earlier became a slow death march. As the game drew to a close, the Braves attempted to muster one last rally in the bottom of the ninth. Mathews led off with a walk, but Crandall and Logan followed with fly-outs. Joe Adcock kept the Braves' hopes alive with a single, but Schoendienst lined out to Mickey Mantle to end the Series. "There is a very narrow line between the team that wins the Series and the one that comes in second," Spahn confessed. "We scored seventeen runs in the first two games, and 25 for the Series. That's it in a nutshell."

> **"There is a very narrow line between the team that wins the Series and the one that comes in second."**
> —WARREN SPAHN

The New York Yankees celebrated on County Stadium's infield after clinching Game Seven of the 1958 Series. (ROBERT KOEHLER COLLECTION)

Eddie Mathews batted just .160 and struck out a record eleven times during the 1958 World Series. (DAVID KLUG COLLECTION)

In a quiet Braves clubhouse the players tried to come to terms with their historic collapse. "We didn't think we could lose two straight in Milwaukee. Maybe that's why we did," Aaron admitted.

Although Billy Bruton led series hitters with a .412 average, the Braves had struck out a record fifty-six times, with eleven of those strikeouts from Eddie Mathews, another record. "The turning point was in our bats. We got eight runs in [the last] five games. . . . Instead of moaning, let's just say how good their pitching was," Haney told reporters in the locker room after the game. With two victories and a save in the Yankees' big comeback, Bob Turley was named the Series' Most Valuable Player.

But even more disturbing than the Braves' Series defeat was the malaise befalling the team and its city. After nearly six years of bliss, the sheen that Major League Baseball had brought to Milwaukee began to tarnish. The players, team officials, civic leaders, and once-devoted fans all knew that Braves baseball had lost its innocence. "It was the beginning of the end of an era in Milwaukee," Donald Davidson concluded.

THE
Plateau
1959–1961

Despite the Braves' 1958 World Series collapse, prognosticators picked them to win a third consecutive pennant in 1959. With a roster that had changed little from the previous two seasons, they looked as solid as ever. But ideological shifts within the organization suggested otherwise, the first being Lou Perini's appointment of Birdie Tebbetts to the Braves front office.

Nicknamed Birdie for his high-pitched voice and talkative nature, George Robert Tebbetts spent fourteen years as an All-Star catcher with the Tigers and Red Sox before he was named the Redlegs' manager in 1954. Tebbetts led Cincinnati to only one first-division finish before being fired late in the 1958 season with the team again in last place. "During Tebbetts' managing tour with Cincinnati, the Braves and Redlegs developed quite a rivalry, which included several bean ball exchanges and brawls," Braves historian Gary Caruso recounted in *The Braves Encyclopedia*. "The Braves' decision to hire Tebbetts as executive vice-president in the fall of 1958 must have seemed rather curious to the Milwaukee players and fans."

When Tebbetts exchanged his cap and jersey for a suit and tie, Braves general manager John Quinn was without a clear role within the organization. "Quinn had been a loyal employee of Lou Perini's for many years, but Tebbetts was brought in basically as Quinn's boss," third baseman Eddie Mathews explained in his autobiography, *Eddie Mathews and the National Pastime*.

The architect who built the Braves into a National League powerhouse was no longer making the personnel decisions for Perini's franchise. "I never could figure why John Quinn got bounced out of his job," Henry Aaron noted in *Aaron*. "That's what it amounted to, as far as I'm concerned."

The Phillies lured Quinn to Philadelphia with a lucrative salary and the title of

> "We were all moving around like a bunch of King Farouks. We played like we were fat, rich and spoiled."
>
> —HENRY AARON

Warren Spahn (with cap on backward) kept his teammates relaxed with his continual banter and antics. (ROBERT KOEHLER COLLECTION)

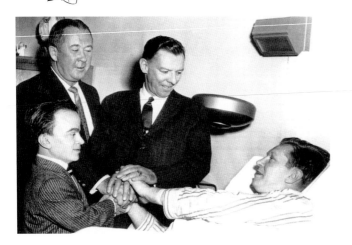

Diagnosed with tuberculosis shortly after the 1958 World Series, Red Schoendienst was visited in the hospital by (from left to right) Braves publicity director Donald Davidson, executive vice president Birdie Tebbetts, and general manager John Quinn. (DAVID KLUG COLLECTION)

vice president. "Many people thought Perini made a big mistake letting Quinn go. He was a good baseball man," Mathews said.

Taking over for Quinn as the Braves' general manager was John McHale, recruited from the Tigers. After a brief playing career, McHale had quickly risen through Detroit's front-office ranks and in 1957, at the age of thirty-five, became the youngest general manager in the game. He was expected to continue the Braves' winning tradition with masterful trades and the nurturing of the team's blossoming farm system.

Tebbetts's and McHale's arrivals and the abrupt departure of John Quinn left manager Fred Haney in a precarious situation. "You can imagine, I guess, what spring training was like, the players not knowing what to expect from Tebbetts or McHale, and wondering what was going on between Haney and Tebbetts," Henry Aaron recalled. "And people told me that Haney and Tebbetts didn't like each other at all."

As former dueling National League managers—with neither too fond of the other's managerial style—Haney and Tebbetts had a tension-filled history. Rumors began circulating that the only way that the Milwaukee skipper would survive past 1959 was to win—not just another National League pennant, but the World Series. The pressure on Haney mounted as the Braves lost nine of their first ten spring training exhibition games. "We were just going through the motions. We were all moving around like a bunch of King Farouks. We played like we were fat, rich and spoiled," Aaron confessed.

Glaringly absent from the Braves' spring training clubhouse was Red Schoendienst. After suffering through a season of deteriorating health, he had been diagnosed with tuberculosis following the 1958 World Series. "Leadership is hard to define," Mathews explained. "Without him we had a real deficiency at second base. If Red had stayed healthy, I really believe we would have run away from the pack in 1959. He made that much of a difference."

Another fan favorite missing from the Braves' spring training dugout was the often-injured Gene Conley. Earlier that spring, John McHale had sent baseball's tallest man to the Phillies because the Braves had an abundance of talented young arms—Joey Jay, Carl Willey, and Juan Pizarro—who were expected to join the established rotation of Spahn, Burdette, Buhl, and Bob Rush.

Back in Milwaukee, preseason ticket sales at County Stadium continued to stagger following the slight dip in 1958's attendance. While the Braves' attendance figures

Red Schoendienst and his clubhouse leadership were sorely missed during the 1959 season. (UWM LIBRARIES, ARCHIVES DEPARTMENT RAINOVIC COLLECTION IMAGE 90)

JOHN
McHALE
NEW BRAVES
GENERAL
MANAGER

General manager John McHale traded in his Detroit Tigers skin for a Milwaukee Braves war bonnet in 1959. (COURTESY MARQUETTE UNIVERSITY ARCHIVES, FRANK J. MARASCO CARTOON COLLECTION)

remained among the highest in the league, the team was no longer breaking records. Milwaukee's fervor for Braves baseball had definitely diminished. Nevertheless, 42,081 Braves fans filled County Stadium on April 14 to see Don McMahon relieve Warren Spahn for the win in an extra-inning home opener against the Phillies.

Milwaukee started the season hot by winning four straight and six of seven. Behind the blistering bats of Eddie Mathews and Henry Aaron, the Braves continued to play good ball into May. When Mathews connected for his fourteenth home run on May 19 to help beat the Cardinals, it put him thirteen games ahead of Babe Ruth's pace to reach sixty home runs in a season. Meanwhile, Aaron was belting the ball at an impressive .468 clip, and it looked as if he'd reach the sacred mark of hitting .400 in a season, last achieved by Ted Williams in 1941. "With those wrists Henry is capable of hitting .400," Fred Haney told reporters, "but don't forget it takes luck as well as ability. The hits have to drop in all year long."

Aaron's luck continued as he hit near .500 well into the season. It seemed no scouting report could pin down his style at the plate. "I think the umpires liked me, because I made their job easy," Aaron confessed. "I would swing at anything in the area code, and I never argued." By midsummer Hammerin' Hank commanded the pitchers' utmost respect, if that can be gauged by how close opposing pitchers were throwing at his head. "I wasn't hit that much," he remembered. "But I got thrown at quite a bit. I hit behind [Eddie] Mathews, who was averaging 40 home runs a year. Back then, when a guy hit a home run, the next guy would go down."

Although he continued to tear up National League pitching, Aaron was continually neglected by the press, while more dramatic playmakers such as Willie Mays, Mickey Mantle, and Roberto Clemente were romanticized in national newspaper headlines. "It's that loping gait of his," Fred Haney explained. "He doesn't look like he's really hustling out there. Then you notice Hank always seems to get up to a fly ball when there's any chance in the world of making the play."

Never one for the spotlight, Aaron prided himself on being a complete ballplayer. "He was never a flashy player," recalled Red Schoendienst. "He just went out and

Braves hurlers (from left to right) Bob Rush, Joey Jay, Carl Willey, Lou Burdette, Warren Spahn, and Bob Buhl helped Milwaukee to the second-best earned run average in the National League in 1959. (ROBERT KOEHLER COLLECTION)

After Harvey Haddix's (pictured) attempt at baseball perfection, Bob Buhl admitted players in Milwaukee's bullpen were stealing Pirates catcher Smoky Burgess's signs and placing a towel on the bullpen fence in such a way to signal fastball or breaking ball to the Braves batters. (ROBERT KOEHLER COLLECTION)

played his game. He picked up his bat and picked up his glove. He went over the lines and played with hardly any fanfare."

Behind Aaron's consistent play, the Braves held a three-game advantage over the Giants by May 26, when they returned to Milwaukee for a fifteen-game home stand. Looking to take the opener against Pittsburgh, Fred Haney loaded his powerful lineup with seven right-handed bats and put ace Lou Burdette on the hill. The Pirates countered with Harvey Haddix, a left-hander sporting a mediocre 3–2 record. As threatening weather limited the County Stadium crowd to just 19,194, Haddix masterfully took the game into the deep innings without a base runner. Even though the Pirates couldn't commandeer a lead, Haddix stifled the hot bats of Aaron, Mathews, and Adcock. After Haddix struck out Andy Pafko, got Johnny Logan to fly out, and sent Lou Burdette down swinging in the bottom of the ninth, he had pitched a perfect game. But since the Pirates had also failed to score, the game was forced into extra innings.

Surviving into the twelfth inning without incident, Haddix made baseball history as he kept pitching on heart and adrenaline. Nobody had ever pitched a no-hit game for more than eleven innings, much less a perfect game for more than nine. The Milwaukee crowd encouraged him with standing ovations after every inning.

Since the Pirates couldn't get to Burdette either, the game continued into the Braves' half of the thirteenth inning—when Braves second baseman Felix Mantilla hit a routine grounder to the Pirates' third baseman Don Hoak. After fielding the ball, Hoak threw it into the dirt, causing it to bounce off first baseman Rocky Nelson's knee. "I'll never forget that play," Haddix acknowledged. "Hoak had all night after picking up the ball. He looked at the seams . . . then he threw it away."

With the perfect game lost, Haddix focused on preserving his no-hitter as Mathews sacrificed Mantilla to second. Then Haddix decided to intentionally walk Aaron and pitch to Adcock. On the second pitch, Adcock connected for a deep drive toward right center that dropped into the bleachers for a home run. In one swift stroke, Haddix had lost his no-hitter and the game. While Adcock circled the bases, he was called out at third, and confusion ensued. Once Mantilla scored, Aaron—who thought the game had officially ended—passed second and turned toward the dugout. "He hadn't seen the ball clear the fence, but he was watching the winning run. All he cared about was winning the game," Mathews explained. Aaron's base-running gaff reduced Adcock's game-winning homer to a game-winning double. The next day National League president Warren Giles ruled that since both runners had been called out—Aaron for leaving the field and Adcock for passing him—the final score should be 1–0. The controversy distracted people from the fact that not only had Harvey Haddix just pitched a perfect game, but Lou Burdette had beat him. "That was the real story," Mathews proclaimed. "Burdette was a sleeper. He never got enough credit for the type of pitcher he was, as good as he was."

A rare base-running mistake by Henry Aaron (center) negated Joe Adcock's (left) homer. (MILWAUKEE JOURNAL SENTINEL)

Skipper Fred Haney was criticized and second-guessed throughout his tenure as the Braves' manager. (WHI IMAGE ID 54480)

Burdette had struck out only two Pirates but hadn't walked anybody. The following winter, he referred to his performance when requesting a raise. "Who pitched the greatest ballgame ever?" Burdette asked during negotiations. "Harvey Haddix," general manager John McHale answered. Pausing only a moment, Burdette replied, "I beat him."

Despite the Braves' holding onto first place in the National League standings for all but one day between May 13 and July 4, a growing faction of critics was questioning the team's leadership. "Haney had been hired to replace the easy-going Charlie Grimm, to bring discipline and firm guidance to a free-spirited, headstrong group of players," Bob Buege asserted in *The Milwaukee Braves: A Baseball Eulogy*. "Under Haney, though, the Braves were not terribly different from the way they had been under Grimm."

Second-guessers from the clubhouse, press box, and grandstands considered Haney's conservative bunting strategies the reason the team couldn't pull away from the rest of the National League pack. "Fred Haney had a different way of managing. I don't think he adapted to the players that we had on the ball club," Eddie Mathews said. "He was going to manage his way regardless of what we had going on out there, and I think that did hurt us."

As rumors of Haney's retirement began to circulate, the Braves' new executive vice president publicly came to his defense. "Ballplayers," Birdie Tebbetts explained to reporters, "are the poorest possible judges of a manager's ability, for the most part. That's because each ballplayer is the central figure in his own little world. Everything rotates around him, and that is how he judges everything, by how it affects his life. A manager has a bigger scope. His life involves every man on his club. The team is important to him, and yet the team is 25 different people, or more."

At the All-Star break, the Braves and Giants were tied atop the National League standings with the Dodgers trailing by only a half game. For 1959's Midsummer Classic, baseball instituted a revolutionary format change to give West Coast fans an All-Star Game of their own. The two All-Star Games were loosely labeled the Eastern Game and the Western Game, and the second game was scheduled for August 3 in Los Angeles. The Braves were well represented in the Eastern Game, played on July 7 in Pittsburgh. Although Mathews was no longer on pace to eclipse Ruth's season home-run total, he was selected as the National League's starting third baseman; joining him in the starting lineup was Henry Aaron, unanimously selected to start by

TOP, LEFT: Johnny Logan enjoyed one of his best seasons at shortstop in 1959 with a .975 fielding average and only eighteen errors. (ROBERT KOEHLER COLLECTION)

TOP, RIGHT: As one of the most mechanically sound catchers of his era, Del Crandall led all National League catchers in 1959 in putouts, assists, double plays, and fielding percentage while making only five errors all season. (ALL-AMERICAN SPORTS, LLC)

MIDDLE: Eddie Mathews led the National League with forty-six home runs in 1959 and was named Wisconsin's athlete of the year. (ROBERT KOEHLER

RIGHT: Red Schoendienst returned for five games during the final month of the 1959 season. (ROBERT KOEHLER COLLECTION)

FAR RIGHT: In 1959 Warren Spahn led the league with twenty-one complete games, tied teammates Lou Burdette and Bob Buhl with four shutouts each, and tied with Burdette and the Giants' Sam Jones for the league lead in wins,

the voting players even though his efforts to hit .400 for the season had cooled. Also featuring Burdette, Crandall, Spahn, and Logan, the National League jumped out to an early lead on a Mathews homer. In the eighth, Aaron singled in the tying run and scored the deciding run after Willie Mays knocked a triple to seal the Nationals' 5–4 victory. In the Western Game, played on August 3 in Los Angeles, the only Braves who saw playing time were Aaron, Mathews, and Crandall; Burdette, Logan, and Spahn rode the pine during the National League's 5–3 loss.

The loss marked the end of a tough streak for the Braves between the All-Star Games. On July 9 Milwaukee and Spahn had lost a thirteen-inning heartbreaker to the Dodgers. The defeat sent the Braves spiraling down the standings with seven consecutive losses. Hoping to reinvigorate the team with some much-needed veteran leadership, general manager John McHale acquired several aging superstars, first trading for former American League batting champion Bobby Avila in late July to fill the absence left by Red Schoendienst. (Despite hitting a game-winning, ninth-inning homer in his first game as a Brave, Avila soon went cold at the plate and would finish the season with a paltry .238 average.) Because Johnny Logan, Eddie Mathews, Wes Covington, and Billy Bruton were nursing late-season injuries, McHale purchased an aging Enos Slaughter from the Yankees, but Slaughter played sparingly in just eleven games.

By September Milwaukee had managed to lose more games than they had won since the All-Star break. With only three weeks left in the season, they sat in third place behind the Dodgers and Giants, and their hopes of repeating as National League champs were slim. "I thought a lot of players were unconsciously sitting back and waiting for someone else to do the job," Frank Torre later told a *Sport* magazine reporter. "A month and a half before the season ended, we suddenly realized that we all had to pitch in and we went out and played baseball."

The Braves won thirteen of their next sixteen games. With a week to go in the regular season, they had reclaimed first place. Several players fed the surge, and nobody in Milwaukee's lineup was hotter than Eddie Mathews, who had connected for eleven homers in the last twenty-five games. Just as important were catcher Del Crandall's contributions from both behind and in front of the plate. "I don't know what we would have done without him," Fred Haney told the press. "He was our clutch hitter. Don't let his average fool you. He's been one of our key guys—a real lifesaver."

After having spent most of the season recovering from tuberculosis, Red Schoendienst rejoined the club for the final pennant push. "He hardly played any at all, but I think that just having him on the bench helped the team get its pride back," Aaron recalled.

On the season's second-to-last day, Milwaukee trailed the first-place Dodgers by a game. Desperate for a win, the Braves again turned to their most seasoned warrior, Warren Spahn. Behind a cannon filled with baseballs that wiggled, sank, curved, and

> "A month and a half before the season ended, we suddenly realized that we all had to pitch in and we went out and played baseball."
>
> —FRANK TORRE

Don McMahon led the senior circuit in 1959 with fifteen saves.
(UWM LIBRARIES, ARCHIVES DEPARTMENT RAINOVIC COLLECTION IMAGE 227)

looked faster than they were, the crafty lefthander handcuffed the Phillies 3–2 for his twenty-first victory of the season. Meanwhile, ninety miles south in Chicago, the Cubs shelled the Dodgers 12–2, creating a first-place tie.

For the fourth year in a row, Milwaukee's season came down to the last possible day, as the Dodgers and Giants were still capable of winning the pennant. But after San Francisco dropped a doubleheader and County Stadium's out-of-town scoreboard posted that the Dodgers had downed the Cubs on September 27, the Braves realized that to stay alive, they'd have to win their season finale against the Phillies. "The situation had certain similarities to 1956, except now we were a game behind instead of a game ahead," Mathews recalled.

Facing the Phillies with no room for error, Bob Buhl kept the game deadlocked at one into the seventh inning. When Milwaukee rallied for three unearned runs in the home half of the seventh, Don McMahon pitched the last two innings to secure the win—his fifteenth save of the year. The Braves had pulled into a regular-season tie with the Dodgers, with an identical 86–68 record. The pennant would be decided in a three-game playoff series, with the winner to face the Chicago White Sox in the World Series. "As far as we were concerned, the hard part was over, because we had survived the pennant race and we were sure—everybody in Milwaukee was sure—that we were the superior team," Aaron said.

Milwaukee hosted the series' first game at County Stadium with only 18,297 fans braving the cold and drizzly weather. "After playing in front of big crowds for so many years, we came to a championship playoff and County Stadium wasn't even half full. It was weird," Eddie Mathews remembered. "Maybe the fans were all waiting for us to play the World Series."

In the Braves' clubhouse, manager Fred Haney faced a dilemma: who to start for Game One. His aces, Spahn and Burdette, needed a rest after pitching practically every day to get the Braves into the postseason. Haney was forced to start the inconsistent Carlton Willey, and the Dodgers immediately took advantage, getting an early run in the first. The Braves rallied for two in the second and forced Los Angeles manager Walter Alston to lift starter Danny McDevitt for rookie reliever Larry Sherry after only one and one-third innings. Sherry held the Braves scoreless for seven and two-thirds innings. When the Dodgers took a 3–2 lead on John Roseboro's solo homer off Willey in the sixth, it was all Los Angeles needed to secure the Game One victory. The Braves were unfazed by their 1–0 series deficit. "On the plane to Los Angeles that night, we were still sure we were going to win it," Aaron professed. "We even sat and talked about how we were going to use our World Series tickets, and who was coming in for the games."

The Los Angeles Coliseum hosted Game Two the following day. With the Braves' pennant hopes hanging in the balance, they sent Lou Burdette to the mound to battle the Dodgers' 1959 National League strikeout king, Don Drysdale. Milwaukee jumped on the Los Angeles hurler for two runs in the top of the first and another in the second. In the bottom of the seventh, with the Braves ahead 4–2, Dodgers left fielder Norm Larker barreled into Johnny Logan while attempting to break up a double play. Though the Braves got both outs, they lost Logan, who was carried off the diamond on a stretcher and replaced by Felix Mantilla. After Milwaukee got another run in the eighth, Burdette entered the bottom of the ninth inning with a 5–2 cushion. "We looked truly superior, like the superior team that we were, all the way into the ninth inning," Aaron recalled.

Johnny Logan was injured in Game Two when the Dodgers' Norm Larker attempted to break up the double play. (NATIONAL BASEBALL HALL OF FAME LIBRARY)

The Dodgers connected for three consecutive singles off Burdette to start the bottom of the ninth. With the bases loaded and nobody out, Haney called on Don Mc-Mahon to quash the mounting rally. "You still had to like our chances with McMahon going," Aaron admitted. "He was big and strong and at the peak of his relief-pitching career then." But Norm Larker greeted the Braves' reliever with a single to left that scored two and brought the tying run to third. Still with nobody out and the lead cut to 5–4, Haney took action. "The sight of Spahn, our ace, warming up in the bullpen was enough to tell me that somebody higher than me was also pretty worried," Aaron observed. Spahn took the mound to retire the first batter he faced. Then pinch hitter Carl Furillo launched a deep pop fly. Aaron speared it with his glove for out number two, but Gil Hodges tagged up from third and tied the score at five.

With the Braves' lead vanquished, their bats remained quiet as the game went into extra innings. The bottom of the twelfth inning found relief specialist Bob Rush looking to extend the game for Milwaukee. But with two outs, Rush yielded a walk to Gil Hodges, and Joe Pignatano followed with a single. Then Furillo connected for a bouncer up the middle that took a high, twisting hop over the second-base bag. Shortstop Felix Mantilla went hard to his right and gloved the ball. Making a quick turn to get the throw to first, Mantilla threw off-balance, and the ball went errantly wide as Hodges hustled around third to score the winning run. "Nobody blamed Felix. It was

Lou Burdette took the mound for Game Two of the 1959 playoffs against the Dodgers hoping he'd clinch his twenty-second win of the year. (UWM LIBRARIES, ARCHIVES DEPARTMENT RAINOVIC COLLECTION IMAGE 82)

just a throw in the dirt that Frank Torre couldn't scoop out. Those things happen," Eddie Mathews remembered.

Convinced all season that no team in the league could touch them, the Braves were left to mope around their clubhouse after the unexpected 6–5 loss. As players changed out of their tomahawk-clad flannel jerseys for the last time that season, the showers echoed. "I've never heard such loud water in my life. It seems that water runs twice as hard and sounds twice as loud in a quiet clubhouse as it does in a happy clubhouse," Aaron said.

Back in Milwaukee, the abundance of fans who once cheered foul balls upon the Braves' arrival in 1953 was noticeably shrinking by 1959. Despite falling just short of their third consecutive World Series, the Braves suffered their second consecutive dip in attendance with only 1.7 million fans. "Maybe the novelty had worn off. I don't know," Mathews reflected years later. "The Braves' season attendance dropped about a quarter-million, but it was still higher than any other team except the Dodgers in that big Coliseum."

Although County Stadium hosted fewer fans, it didn't keep those who attended from being extensively vocal about the team's shortcomings. "The 1959 season had been filled with so much promise that its wrenching finish was difficult to accept," Braves historian Gary Caruso attested.

The discriminating public and press placed most of the blame on manager Fred Haney. Just five days after the season-ending loss, Haney caved in to the pressure and resigned. "I think Haney is the most underrated manager I've known. He belongs with the very best, and he has a record to prove it," declared Braves publicity director Donald Davidson in his autobiography, *Caught Short*. "Over a four-season span, from 1956 through 1959, Fred won two pennants, lost another by a game, and lost a fourth in a playoff."

Several of the Braves' veterans came to their manager's defense, including Warren Spahn. "We had better take stock of ourselves and give some thought as to why we didn't win the pennant instead of just blaming the manager," he told reporters. "I don't think it was Haney's fault. I thought he did a good job."

Outfielder Wes Covington agreed. "Remember, Haney didn't build this club; it was here when he came," he commented to the press. "If we had

Fred Haney (pictured left with owner Lou Perini) had the highest winning percentage of any manager in baseball during his time with the Braves between 1956 and 1959. (WHI IMAGE ID 49325)

won the pennant, nobody would have said anything about bunting or running. Maybe there are things he could have done different, but he should be given credit where credit is due."

Others were quick to applaud Haney's departure, including the Braves' often brash but passionate shortstop. "When they announced Haney was out, you can bet few players were sorry," Johnny Logan was quoted in the *New York Post*. "Anybody could manage with what we had. We should have won by ten games."

With Haney gone and absentee owner Lou Perini spending less and less time in Milwaukee, the brunt of the fans' discontent quickly shifted to the Braves' front office. It was especially evident in the newspaper editorials, in which fans voiced their frustration about Bostonian Lou Perini becoming an "absentee owner" and suggested

Immediately following Fred Haney's departure, speculation spread about a likely replacement. (UWM LIBRARIES, ARCHIVES DEPARTMENT RAINOVIC COLLECTION IMAGE 89)

Logan. Dashing in to scoop it up, Logan rifled a throw to first baseman Joe Adcock. The ball sailed a bit wide, but Adcock grabbed the throw with his foot on the bag for the out. After the game, Spahn had to credit Burdette. "If he hadn't pitched his no-hitter, I don't think I would have gotten mine," Spahn joked with reporters. "When Lou pitched his, I just had to go out there and pitch one myself."

Despite the two late-season no-hitters from Burdette and Spahn, Milwaukee's pennant hopes never rebounded from the team's devastating August. Their second-place finish with an 88–66 record was seven games behind the eventual world champion Pittsburgh Pirates. Dressen had delivered on two of his preseason promises: the Braves won more games than the year before, and they finished six games ahead of the Dodgers. But it was small consolation; the Braves' season attendance continued to decline. For the second straight year, a disturbingly new low was established in Milwaukee as fewer than 1.5 million customers paid to watch the Braves play at County Stadium. It was concrete evidence that the "Milwaukee Miracle" was over.

◆ ◆ ◆

After their disappointing second-place finish in 1960, the Braves spent their off-season dismantling their roster of core players. "We were all getting older. It was inevitable that something like that would happen, but you still hate to see it happen," Eddie Mathews admitted. "Ever since the Braves moved from Boston, our lineup had been pretty much the same, very consistent." Realizing the roster still possessed trade value, general manager John McHale focused on bolstering the team's infield defense. To receive All-Star second baseman Frank Bolling from Detroit, the Braves sent away one of Milwaukee's first heroes, Billy Bruton. "That was the first real sign that John McHale was going to clean house," Mathews said.

But McHale's savvy trade for Bolling was overshadowed by his decision to deal away pitchers Joey Jay and Juan Pizarro after the organization labeled them as under-achievers. "What really hurt was losing the young Braves," Henry Aaron noted in his 1991 autobiography. "I've always felt that we would have won some more championships if we had held on to Pizarro and Jay."

In return for Pizarro and Jay, Milwaukee got two-time All-Star and three-time Gold Glove Award–winning shortstop Roy McMillan. "He wasn't much with the stick, but he could play shortstop with the best of them," Mathews remembered. To make room for Bolling, McHale gave second baseman Red Schoendienst his unconditional release—to the dismay of many of the players. "That move made no sense to us," Mathews said. "They didn't trade him for anybody; they just let him go."

With McMillan assuming the everyday shortstop duties, Johnny Logan became expendable, and McHale traded him to Pittsburgh at midseason for outfielder Gino

After thirteen seasons as a fixture at shortstop in Milwaukee—five with the Brewers, eight with the Braves—Johnny Logan was traded to the Pirates for journeyman outfielder Gino Cimoli. (ROBERT KOEHLER COLLECTION)

During the Braves 1961 spring training, several Wisconsin natives attempted to make the opening day roster, including (clockwise from bottom left) Dennis Overby, Dave Fracaro, John Braun, Clair Hickman, Bob Botz, and Bob Uecker. (ROBERT KOEHLER COLLECTION)

Cimoli. It was a loss that would be felt by both players and fans. Henry Aaron noted, "Johnny was great for team spirit, the most humorous man I ever played with."

Realizing Wes Covington was never going to be the answer in left field, McHale acquired three-time All-Star Frank Thomas from the Cubs. "He hit quite a few home runs for us and gave us help in the outfield, which we needed," Mathews said. "Then after the season the people upstairs sent him to the Mets. What their thinking was, I have no idea. John McHale did a lot of things I never understood."

By spring training McHale had assembled a team vastly different from the one of years past. "The Braves' personality was being changed to match the desires of the new personality of the front office: Tebbetts, McHale and Dressen," Aaron acknowledged.

As the outsiders and transients replaced the familiar faces in the Braves clubhouse, Milwaukee's biggest change during 1961's spring training was the players' new housing arrangements. "That happened to be the first spring camp in which the Milwaukee Braves wanted every player on the team to stay together—black and white players alike," Joe Torre remembered. According to Torre, this didn't suit the Braves' usual exclusive hotel in Bradenton, and they moved to the nearby Twilight Hotel in Palmetto, and "even there they had to feed us in a private room where no one else could see blacks and whites eating together."

In addition to rooming and eating together, the Braves ordered all race signs dropped at their Bradenton ballpark. "I wish I could say that we were a better team with segregation behind us, but the fact is that while we were coming together off the field, we were coming apart on it," Aaron confessed.

Back in Milwaukee, a war was brewing—one that divided a city from its ball club. "The people on the county board, which

Restless Braves support-
ers hoped the team's
off-season roster tinkering
would brew up another
pennant for Milwaukee
in 1961. (COURTESY
MARQUETTE UNIVERSITY
ARCHIVES, FRANK J. MARASCO
CARTOON COLLECTION)

controlled the stadium, got greedy," Mathews said. "They decided they could make some money by banning carry-ins and making the fans buy beer from the concession stands and vendors, at a big mark-up, of course."

The already-apathetic fans—many of whom worked at the local breweries—found the ban insulting. The first indication that the beer carry-in ban had alienated even the most devoted of fans came on the chilly afternoon of April 11, when County Stadium was only two-thirds full for the Opening Day game against the Cardinals. Just 33,327 fans were in attendance to watch Warren Spahn lose a 2–1 heartbreaker in the tenth inning.

On April 23 the seemingly ageless Spahn celebrated his fortieth birthday by beating the Pirates for his 289th career victory. Five days later, Spahn was set to face the San Francisco Giants and one of

Fans were left to their own
devices after alcohol was
banned at County Stadium
in spring 1961. (MILWAUKEE
JOURNAL SENTINEL)

the most potent slugging crews in the National League. "I knew my arm and I knew my hitters," Spahn said, "and as I lost sheer speed, I went for variety." Another anemic County Stadium crowd of 8,518 watched Spahn mow down the Giants' Willie Mays, Willie McCovey, Felipe Alou, Harvey Kuenn, and Orlando Cepeda with a mixture of screwballs and sliders. The Braves took an early first-inning lead, which was all the southpaw needed, as he went on to face the minimum twenty-seven batters in the Braves' 1–0 victory. Striking out nine while allowing only a pair of walks that were erased by double plays, Spahn became the second-oldest man to hurl a no-hitter in major-league history, behind Cy Young. "It was so easy, it was pathetic," Spahn remembered. "Everything went my way, and they kept guessing wrong. But let's just face it; I was just plain lucky." After going nearly sixteen seasons without a no-hitter, Spahn had pitched two within a span of six starts. "Here I waited nearly a lifetime to get my no-hitter, and no sooner do I get it than I come up with another. That's life."

Two days later a meager crowd of 13,114 dragged itself to the ballpark for the series-deciding rubber match against the Giants. With Willie Mays in an 0-for-7 slump, the Braves looked ready to reclaim the National League's top spot. Mays had played through a stomachache all weekend but was feeling better by Sunday. By the end of the day, the Giants had throttled the Braves 14–4, setting a National League record of eight home runs—four off Mays's bat. "You're satisfied if you get two in a game, but when you get three, that's something you never expect," Mays confessed to reporters after the game. "Four? That's like reaching for the moon."

The Braves continued to play mediocre ball, flirting with .500 through most of May. By the end of the month, they sat in fifth place at 19–20, already five and a half games out of first. Nagging injuries began to catch up with Milwaukee, beginning with catcher Del Crandall, whose hampered throwing shoulder landed him on the disabled list. "Losing Del hurt us. He was an all-star practically every year and a strong influence on our pitching staff," Mathews said.

Instead of instigating a trade, John McHale turned to Milwaukee's farm system and called up a pudgy catcher from the same home in Brooklyn that had provided defensive standout first baseman Frank Torre. After winning the batting title with the team's minor-league affiliate in Eau Claire, Joe Torre and his hot bat became the Braves salvation behind the plate. "[Del Crandall's] backup, Charlie Lau, who became a famous hitting coach, had been filling in, but now it looked as if Crandall would be out longer than the Braves first thought," Torre recalled. Since he had hung out in the clubhouse with his older brother Frank, Joe immediately fit in with the veteran-filled roster. "Spahn and Burdette were . . . like older brothers. They used to take me to the movies with them in the afternoon and to restaurants at night. Dressen, however, wasn't too hot about me striking up a friendship with them. 'Don't hang around Spahn and Burdette,' he'd say. 'They're like the Katzenjammer Kids.'"

> "Here I waited nearly a lifetime to get my no-hitter, and no sooner do I get it than I come up with another. That's life."
> —WARREN SPAHN

THE Descent
1962-1964

Lou Perini's vision that Major League Baseball would expand into hungry metropolises far beyond the East Coast exploded into a baseball-wide revolution by 1962. In less than a decade, six of the original sixteen teams were playing in different cities. America's Pastime had become a sport of franchises competing for financial gain. The Braves' instant success in the untapped market of Milwaukee was directly responsible for the Browns moving to Baltimore in 1954, the Athletics going to Kansas City in 1955, and the Senators moving to Minnesota in 1961. The Braves' impressive profits led Horace Stoneham to move the Giants to San Francisco and sent Walter O'Malley's Dodgers to Los Angeles in 1958. Although critics feared that one of the sport's foundations—the bond between a city and its baseball team—had been destroyed, the franchise relocations instead proved that America had an unquenched thirst for its favorite pastime, evidenced by shattered attendance records throughout both leagues. In addition, the success of the Braves' relocation from Boston to Milwaukee was the catalyst for baseball's newfound priority to operate as a profit-motivated big business.

In the weeks following the departure of the Dodgers and Giants to California, the clamor for major-league expansion grew into a contentious coast-to-coast roar. If cities that weren't able to cajole one of the existing sixteen franchises—including Toronto, Atlanta, Denver, Houston, Dallas, and Minneapolis—couldn't join Major League Baseball, they threatened to organize a third major circuit, the Continental League. To defuse this creation of a competing league, in 1961 the American League expanded from eight to ten teams with the addition of the Los Angeles Angels and the Washington Senators, and in 1962 the National League added the New York Metropolitans and Houston Colt .45s.

Attendance was sparse at best by May 1962. (MILWAUKEE JOURNAL SENTINEL)

The early prognosis was grim for the Braves' pennant hopes during their 1962 spring training camp. (COURTESY MARQUETTE UNIVERSITY ARCHIVES, FRANK J. MARASCO CARTOON COLLECTION)

With new teams and more contests, both leagues increased their traditional schedule of 154 games to 162 and pared down the number of games teams played against each other from 22 to 18. The once-rhythmic baseball schedule of four-game series was replaced with three-game series, and more games would be played under lights. Ultimately, expansion provided baseball owners eight additional dates to add to their bottom line.

Other cities wanted to reap major-league rewards. Nearly a thousand miles south of Milwaukee, Atlanta, Georgia, was growing into an urban metropolis complete with gleaming skyscrapers and snarled freeways. Using the blueprint Milwaukee had designed nearly a decade earlier, in 1961 newly elected Atlanta mayor Ivan Allen Jr. promised to bring Major League Baseball to the South—even if he had to lure a team from elsewhere. "One of the planks in Allen's platform . . . was the construction of a sports stadium," author Furman Bisher recounted in *Miracle in Atlanta*. "[But] after [he] had been mayor for more than a year, Atlanta still sat there without a stadium and with no apparent motivation to get one started."

Back in Milwaukee, owner Lou Perini—well aware that his team had lost much of its turnstile appeal—finally made an agreement with Milwaukee's WTMJ television station to broadcast fifteen of the Braves' 1962 road games. Baseball's evolution into a big business was creating new revenue streams, and the hundreds of thousands of dollars the Braves would receive in sponsorship and advertising money offset Perini's fears of television cutting into ticket revenues.

In Bradenton, Birdie Tebbetts, the once fiery and controversial manager of the rival Cincinnati Reds, looked to bring a less contentious atmosphere to the Braves clubhouse during spring training. Donald Davidson, recently promoted to traveling secretary, wrote later, "When Tebbetts joined the Braves as a vice-president and shifted to the dugout as manager in 1961, he ceased being a villain. Even the Braves who had despised him in Cincy liked him in Milwaukee. He was strict with the players, frequently leveling fines, but at the end of the season he'd take the money and pitched a party for the team, buying presents for the players."

General manager John McHale, on the other hand, seemed ready to all but sacrifice the team's future after having spent another off-season attempting to refurbish

Crews from Milwaukee's WTMJ-TV began televising road games during the 1962 season. (MILWAUKEE JOURNAL SENTINEL)

the Braves roster with savvy trades and signings. To acquire pitcher Bob Shaw from Kansas City, Milwaukee parted with three of its brightest prospects—Joe Azcue, Ed Charles, and Manny Jimenez—all of whom went on to have respectable major-league careers. In a lopsided trade with the Cubs, McHale gave up Bob Buhl—who went on to win twelve games for Chicago—for underachieving junk thrower Jack Curtis, who collected only four wins in 1962. Baseball's expansion draft, held in the fall of 1961 to fill the new teams' rosters, left the Braves with several of its players unprotected and available to fill the rosters of the newly formed New York Mets and Houston Colt .45s franchises. Felix Mantilla was lost to the Mets and was soon joined by Frank Thomas, who amassed thirty-four home runs and ninety-four runs batted in during the Mets' hapless inaugural season. "There's no telling what he'd have done if he'd been surrounded by the sluggers the Braves possessed," Braves historian Gary Caruso said of Thomas's potential in Milwaukee.

The one position that benefited from the Braves' youth movement was that of catcher. Uncertain whether Del Crandall would overcome the nagging injuries that hampered his throwing arm, the club looked to primary backups Joe Torre and Bob Uecker, a Milwaukeean who would become more famous for his comedic wit than his backstop skills. "I would be hailed as the first Milwaukee native to play for the Braves," Bob Uecker wrote in his autobiography, *Catcher in the Wry*. "Later, I would be hailed as the first Milwaukee native to be traded by the Braves. Hometown boy makes good."

LEFT: General manager John McHale acquired Bob Shaw (left) in hopes he could bring some youth to an aging pitching staff that still featured Warren Spahn and Lou Burdette. (ROBERT KOEHLER COLLECTION)

RIGHT: Milwaukee native Bob Uecker joined an already talented Braves catching corps that featured Del Crandall and Joe Torre. (DAVID KLUG COLLECTION)

Artist Al Rainovic captured the fans' growing disinterest in attending Braves games at County Stadium. (UWM LIBRARIES, ARCHIVES DEPARTMENT RAINOVIC COLLECTION IMAGE 271)

"The Braves . . . had become the one thing baseball fans can't accept. A mediocre team."

—BOB UECKER

For the fifth year in a row, the Braves' preseason ticket sales stalled. Whether fans were disgruntled over the County Stadium beer ban or the departure of crowd pleasers, they were no longer interested in going to the ballpark. "When I joined them," Uecker confessed, "the Braves had declined from their World Series years, '57 and '58, and had become the one thing baseball fans can't accept. A mediocre team. Not good enough to compete, not bad enough to be lovable."

With a roster made up of aging superstars, inferior replacements, and underachieving prospects, the Braves started the season with a seven-game road trip—and dropped their first five games. By the time Warren Spahn took the mound for County Stadium's home opener on April 18, the club had a pitiful 1–6 record. In the wake of the worst start in franchise history, Milwaukee hosted its smallest Opening Day turnout; only 30,001 watched the Braves rally for four runs in the bottom of the eighth to beat the Giants. The empty seats were a clear indication that the fans weren't interested in the team's efforts, and as the season progressed, crowds under 10,000 soon were the norm rather than the exception.

By May 9 Milwaukee sat nine games out of first in seventh place with a 10–14 record. The smallest crowd in County Stadium history, 3,673 stalwarts, sat in thirty-eight-degree weather to watch the Braves beat the Pirates. The next night Milwaukee dropped a 4–3 decision to Pittsburgh in front of only 2,746. "Every night at County Stadium, it was like playing in front of your closest friends," Joe Torre said.

Relegated to a backup role with the return of Del Crandall, Torre seemed to be the only one benefiting from the early-season weather conditions. "I became a cold-weather catcher," Torre admitted in his autobiography, *Chasing the Dream*. "If Tebbetts thought it was too cold to risk Crandall's cranky shoulder, he'd start me instead."

On the diamond, the Braves' growing futility manifested itself against one of the worst teams in baseball history: the expansion New York Mets. Only four days after Tebbetts sold reliever Don McMahon to Houston because he felt the right-hander had lost his fastball, the Mets swept Milwaukee in a doubleheader, with both game-winning home runs coming in the ninth inning. Eight days later, the Mets swept another doubleheader at County Stadium after the Braves blew leads in both games. The Mets earned their sixth win in ten games against the Braves, 6–5, at the Polo Grounds on June 19. With a 17–45 record, they had more than one-third of their wins against Tebbets's club.

Led by Henry Aaron's 45 round-trippers, the Braves feast-or-famine offense in 1962 finished with 181 home runs, good for second best in the National League. But their .252 batting average ranked a lowly eighth; only the expansion Colt .45s and Mets had lower averages. (AUTHOR'S COLLECTION)

RIGHT: In June 1962 Milwaukee's County Board once again permitted fans to carry beer into County Stadium. (COURTESY OF MIKE RODELL)

In Milwaukee, attendance continued to nosedive as the Braves dipped closer to the National League cellar. To lure fans, the ball club rescinded the beer carry-in ban on June 8, but that did little to boost long-term attendance figures.

Despite disappointing turnouts, Lou Perini publicy denied rumors that he was interested in selling the Braves. "Perini at that time hardly ever came to Milwaukee to see the ballclub," third baseman Eddie Mathews remembered. "He just let McHale run the show while he tended to his construction business back east." While insisting that the team wasn't for sale, Perini placed 1.5 million shares of stock on the open market. "The ballplayers never paid much attention to any of that stuff, one way or the other," Mathews said, "but

we did notice something": a group of businessmen who frequented County Stadium during the 1962 season. "These guys started showing up at our games, and that was when we were hearing all this happy crap about Perini wanting out."

By the first All-Star Game, played in Washington, DC, on July 10, the Braves were 42–43, fourteen games behind the league leaders. Milwaukee was well represented, with Henry Aaron, Frank Bolling, Del Crandall, Eddie Mathews, Bob Shaw, and Warren Spahn on the National League roster. President John Kennedy threw out the first pitch before the Nationals pulled out an exciting 3–1 victory, with Bob Shaw earning the save. On July 30 the All-Star squads faced off again, this time in Wrigley Field, and the American League trumped the Nationals 9–4.

Following the year's first All-Star Game, Milwaukee began to play respectable baseball as a resurgent Warren Spahn continued as the team's anchor. "His snapping fastball was gone, but he could still beat them with his off-speed pitches and his control and his head," Uecker wrote. After blasting his thirty-first career round-tripper on July 26 against the Mets to establish a National League record for most home runs hit by a pitcher, Spahn focused on becoming the winningest left-handed pitcher in baseball history.

Spahn took the mound against the Pittsburgh Pirates on September 29 as if it were just another game. But as the game entered the late innings, his unsmiling seriousness on the mound intensified. Merely cocking his head to one side while preparing for each pitch, the forty-one-year-old fed off the anxious Pirates hitters. "Some-

Warren Spahn led the Braves pitching staff with eighteen wins in 1962 while posting a respectable 3.04 ERA and leading the league with twenty-two complete games. (COURTESY OF BOB BUEGE)

times I get behind on batters deliberately," Spahn confessed. "Makes them hungry for fat pitches. I made a living on hungry hitters."

The Braves' bats provided enough punch behind home runs from Joe Adcock and rookie Tommie Aaron as Spahn clinched his 327th career win with the 7–3 victory. Upon becoming the most successful left-hander in baseball history, the great southpaw credited his longevity with staying healthy. "I never went in the trainer's room," he explained. "I didn't believe in icing my arm after a game. Ice is for mixed drinks, not your arm. All I'd do is go in the shower and let the hot water run down my arm."

The Braves closed out the 1962 season the next day with an uninspired loss to Pittsburgh. Posting a respectable 86–76 record, the team nevertheless finished in fifth place, a distant fifteen and a half games behind the Giants. With their lowest winning percentage since arriving in Milwaukee, the Braves placed in the National League's first division only because the Mets and Colt .45s had expanded the league to ten teams. Five days after the end of the 1962 season, Birdie Tebbetts abruptly resigned.

Two weeks later the Braves' tumultuous off-season began when John McHale hired Bobby Bragan as the team's next skipper. "Instead of a transfusion of young blood and fresh talent, we got a new manager with an ego problem," Eddie Mathews said.

The most notorious incident behind Bragan's boisterous reputation happened on July 31, 1957, in front of County Stadium fans. In the second unsuccessful year of his first big-league managing job for Pittsburgh, Bragan made an appeal play at second base, claiming Milwaukee base runner Bob Buhl had missed second base. "When the

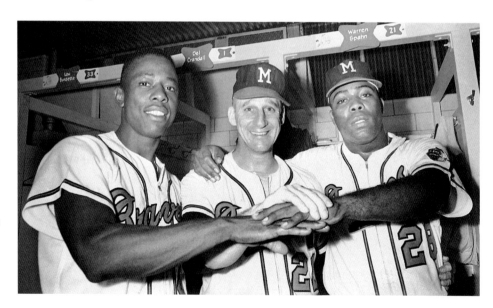

In 1962, Henry Aaron and his younger brother Tommie (right) established themselves in the major-league record books after the two homered in the same inning, a feat not performed since 1938 by the Waner brothers. (WHI IMAGE ID 49387)

Despite being a former major-league catcher, Braves manager Birdie Tebbetts struggled with a pitching staff that didn't post a twenty-game winner for the first time since 1955, and a bullpen that lost thirty-two one-run games in 1962. (ROBERT KOEHLER COLLECTION)

> "Ice is for mixed drinks, not your arm."
> –WARREN SPAHN

umpire ruled in the Braves' favor, Bragan displayed his opinion by holding his nose. That prompted his ejection," Gary Caruso recounted in *The Braves Encyclopedia*. Instead of walking off the field gracefully, Bragan paraded back onto the field, sipping an orange drink he had purchased from the stands. After offering a sip to umpire Frank Secory, he was ordered off the field. He then motioned as if to throw the drink into the umpire's face. Only under threat of Pittsburgh's forfeit of the game did Bragan finally leave the field. Two days after the incident, he was fired.

Even with a new manager in place, Lou Perini saw a bleak future for the franchise. Although he had reaped $7.5 million in profits during his first nine years in Milwaukee, the Braves owner posted his first losses in 1962. The fans were avoiding County Stadium in record numbers, and the team's total 1962 attendance of 766,921 had them finishing ninth out of ten National League clubs—a 30 percent decline from the previous year. Perini decided it was time to get out of the baseball business.

On November 16, 1962, Lou Perini and his Perini Corporation, which had held controlling interest in the team since 1944, sold the Milwaukee Braves to the LaSalle Corporation, a group of prominent Chicago-area businessmen led by thirty-four-year-old insurance broker William Bartholomay. At a press conference Lou Perini enthusiastically introduced the new owners as "young sportsmen who are more interested in winning a pennant than in financial returns." But former Milwaukee Brewers owner and Perini rival Bill Veeck sensed, "The whole deal had the uncomfortable smell of city slickers coming in to take over." *Milwaukee Journal*

The Braves' once-royal robe was in need of refurbishment by the end of the 1962 season. (COURTESY MARQUETTE UNIVERSITY ARCHIVES, FRANK J. MARASCO CARTOON COLLECTION)

Lou Perini (left) enthusiastically introduced the Braves' new ownership group at a press conference. (COURTESY OF BOB BUEGE)

sports editor Oliver Kuechle soon dubbed the new owners "The Rover Boys," possibly after an early 1900s children's book series featuring three mischievous brothers.

Bartholomay and his partners were heirs to the family fortunes of Johnson's Floor Wax, Searle Pharmaceuticals, the Miller Brewing Company, and Chicago's Palmer House. They had focused their efforts on Milwaukee after an unsuccessful attempt to purchase the Chicago White Sox a few years earlier.

Introductions were in order after the Braves' ownership and field general changed during the off-season. (UWM LIBRARIES, ARCHIVES DEPARTMENT RAINOVIC COLLECTION IMAGE 41)

During the early months of 1963, few certificates were issued during the Braves stock drive. (DAVID KLUG COLLECTION)

> "The golden years were over and the team was no longer winning pennants."
>
> —DONALD DAVIDSON

Purchasing all but 10 percent of the Braves for $6,218,480, the Braves' new owners had a $2 million balloon payment due in 1968. Desperate to generate a new revenue stream and eliminate fears of absentee ownership, Bartholomay and his associates offered to sell 115,000 shares of team stock at a price of ten dollars per share to Wisconsin residents before the 1963 season. The new owners hoped the stock sale would not only pull the team back above the financial break-even point but also reinvigorate fan interest. The invitation to Milwaukee buyers was widely advertised—and largely ignored. "If there had been a market for it, the club would probably still be in Milwaukee," Donald Davidson concluded, "but the golden years were over and the team was no longer winning pennants."

By April 7 only thirteen thousand shares had been sold to just sixteen hundred new investors. The stock offering was deemed a bust and was withdrawn. Followed by a preseason ticket sales push that exposed the community's local apathy with even fewer season tickets sold than in years prior, the rookie owners sensed they had bought into a grave situation. Citing the failed stock sale, Bartholomay's ownership group claimed Milwaukee no longer wanted the Braves. They immediately began looking for a new, more hospitable venue for their franchise. "We never considered the possibility of the Braves leaving town," Henry Aaron said. "But the Miracle of Milwaukee, like hula hoops and ducktail haircuts, had been left behind in the fifties."

◆ ◆ ◆

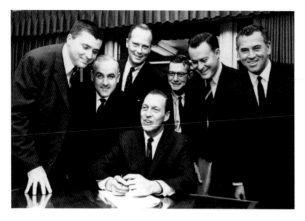

With the new ownership syndicate overseeing his personnel moves, newly promoted president and general manager John McHale (seated) continued to dismantle the Braves' aging roster prior to the start of the 1963 season. (COURTESY OF BOB BUEGE)

> "From the first day Bobby [Bragan] arrived, he was going to do things his own way."
>
> –HENRY AARON

During the off-season, newly promoted president and general manager John McHale continued dismantling the team's aging roster, including sending Joe Adcock to Cleveland. "A Braves fan returning to County Stadium after, say, a four-year absence would have been hard-pressed to identify the Milwaukee players," baseball historian Bob Buege said in *The Milwaukee Braves: A Baseball Eulogy.* "Fortunately for that fan and others like him, the Braves began wearing their names on the back of their uniforms in 1963." The extensive roster turnover, along with jersey alterations that included the elimination of the tomahawk, made fans feel management was attempting to generate a new team identity in the wake of the ownership change.

The Braves also abandoned their traditional Bradenton, Florida, spring training facilities for a new state-of-the-art facility across the state in West Palm Beach. "Mr. Perini was in the process of building up an entire side of the city—I remember him taking me around in his car and telling me what he was going to do with all that swampland—and a major part of the development was a new spring facility for the Braves," Henry Aaron recalled in his autobiography *I Had a Hammer: The Hank Aaron Story.* According to Aaron, when Perini sold the Braves to the LaSalle Corporation, "part of the deal was that the team would train on his swampland."

The new facility included one full diamond and an additional half field for infield work, all providing skipper Bobby Bragan the perfect arena for molding the Braves into winners. "From the first day Bobby arrived, he was going to do things his own way," Aaron said.

Bragan often lashed out in frustration at his team of veterans on the decline. "He could really get on your case. He had a way of talking out of the side of his mouth, like Humphrey Bogart, and he could dust you off equally well with a sarcastic line or with your basic seaman's vocabulary," Bob Uecker recalled.

With pressure from management to quickly rebuild the team into a winner, the Braves' new manager was decisive about who would make it out of spring training. "We had the feeling Bobby Bragan was there as a hatchet man," Warren Spahn said. "Getting rid of veterans was his role."

Pitcher Carl Willey was the first big name jettisoned at the end of camp, when he was sent to the Mets. Soon after, Bragan focused on the Braves' backstop dilemma. "When the '63 season began, Del Crandall was still first-string catcher," Bragan recounted in his autobiography, *You Can't Hit the Ball with the Bat on Your Shoulder.* "He'd had many great years with the Braves, a good handler of pitchers who handled the bat well enough to hit second in the lineup—rare for a catcher, but it quickly became clear in '63 that Joe Torre was simply younger and better than Del." By the end of spring training, Bragan had made Torre his starting catcher.

By then Bragan's unyielding ego had already created strained relationships with several of the veterans. "Bobby probably knew as much baseball as any of the Braves managers, but he had difficulty communicating with players. Bragan, as a manager, was a complex man," Donald Davidson wrote.

As controversial as he was stubborn, Bragan often made decisions based on emotion. "I'm sure I would have been a better manager if I hadn't been influenced by a ballplayer's personality," he said years later. "Players' attitudes and off-the-field habits sometimes affected my treatment of them." With the Braves scheduled to open the season on the road in Pittsburgh, Bragan assigned the honorary Opening Day pitching duties to Lou Burdette instead of Warren Spahn. "I'd like to think I let Lou pitch the first game because he'd been so outstanding during spring training, but the truth is I probably felt he deserved the honor over Spahn because of their difference in attitude," he confessed. "Warren Spahn's single interest was Warren Spahn."

Burdette and the Braves couldn't get the job done in Pittsburgh, and they started the season winless at 0–2. Only 26,120 fans were at County Stadium's home opener on April 11 to behold Warren Spahn's dominance of the Mets. Except for a Duke Snider home run, no Met got past second base during the Braves' 6–1 victory. "Despite the fact that the team was falling apart around him, old Hooks was as good as ever in 1963," Henry Aaron proclaimed.

Following Spahn's 328th career victory, Bragan's Braves continued to streak their way through April. A four-game losing streak followed a seven-game winning streak, and Milwaukee finished the month with a 12–8 record, good for third place and only two and a half games out of first. Bragan seemed to have assembled a solid combination of veterans and youth, all of them hungry to capture another pennant. "In '63 I was having a great time," rookie infielder Denis Menke fondly recalled. "I was glad I was breaking into the major leagues with guys like Spahn and Mathews and Crandall. That season we used to have team parties and everyone would be there."

Meanwhile, nearly eight hundred miles south of Milwaukee, Atlanta mayor Ivan Allen Jr. continued his quest for a major-league franchise. When disgruntled Kansas City Athletics owner Charlie

Bobby Bragan's complex approach to managing baseball games left many of the Braves frustrated, confused, or bored during moments of instruction. (ROBERT KOEHLER COLLECTION)

Finley came to Atlanta on April 25, Allen looked to entice him to move his franchise south. The mayor's tour through the "Heart of the South" led them to a pile of rubble near the Georgia state capitol, less than a mile from Atlanta's downtown district. According to Furman Bisher in *Miracle in Atlanta: The Atlanta Braves Story*, Mayor Allen gushed: "Just like I told you, Mr. Finley. The greatest site for a sports stadium in America." Finley replied, "I can almost hear the crack of the bat. You build a stadium here, and I guarantee you Atlanta will get a major league franchise." With that brief exchange, Allen had created the momentum necessary for the city to build a major-league-caliber stadium on speculation.

> "I was starting to feel like a stranger on my own ball club."
>
> —EDDIE MATHEWS

Back in Milwaukee, the Braves' promising season quickly began to disintegrate. Finishing May in eighth place, Milwaukee was five games under .500 and eight and a half games out of first. Only the hapless Colt .45s and Mets kept them out of the National League cellar. With the team struggling, John McHale decided Lou Burdette was on the downside of his career and deemed him expendable. After thirteen seasons and 173 wins in Braves flannels, the man radio announcer Earl Gillespie called Loober was dealt to the Cardinals—along with his unsubstantiated pitching secrets. "Burdette never told me or anybody else on the team what substance he used or where he stashed it when he threw his illegal pitch," Joe Torre speculated in his memoir, *Chasing the Dream*. "He knew if he told a teammate about his secret and that person was traded, the word would be all over the league."

Burdette's departure marked the end of his pitching duo with Spahn, a combination that had produced 443 victories for the Braves. And it left the team with even fewer familiar faces on the bench. "With Buhl and now Old Nitro leaving as well, I was starting to feel like a stranger on my own ball club," Mathews said in *Eddie Mathews and the National Pastime*. "The only ones left from the old days were Spahnie and I and Crandall, and of course Aaron."

As the last of the Braves aces from the team's championship years, Spahn was left to lead a staff of young hurlers expected to quickly develop into winners. Denny Lemaster, Bob Hendley, Tony Cloninger, Claude Raymond, and Bob Sadowski all showed natural ability but lacked the consistency that had symbolized Milwaukee's hurlers during their glory years. It was no surprise, then, that on July 2, Spahn was given the task of facing Juan Marichal during another inclement evening in San Francisco.

Just 15,921 fans braved the San Francisco chill to witness what would become one of the last truly great heavyweight pitching matchups in baseball history with both hurlers going the distance in a baseball marathon for the ages. Marichal, the Giants' twenty-five-year-old right-hander, and Spahn, the forty-two-year-old Braves southpaw, cut through their opposing lineups inning after inning, leaving little behind on the base paths. As the innings mounted, the scoring opportunities withered. The game remained scoreless as it marched into extra innings. Finally, in the bottom

The Braves' John McHale with 1963 All-Star Game representatives Joe Torre and Warren Spahn (ROBERT KOEHLER COLLECTION)

of the sixteenth, the odds caught up with Spahn, who until now had kept Willie Mays hitless. With one out, Mays sent one of Spahn's trademark screwballs into the night to defeat the Braves 1–0. In a remarkable feat of stamina, both pitchers went the distance, as Marichal allowed just eight hits in sixteen innings and struck out ten while Spahn gave up nine hits in fifteen and one-third innings. "Both pitchers threw over 200 pitches. Can you imagine any pitcher going sixteen innings anymore?" Mathews pondered nearly thirty years later. "And what about the catcher? Del Crandall worked that whole game."

The outcome of the epic pitching duel was just one of many disappointments during the first half of the season, and the Braves found themselves seven games behind the first-place Dodgers at 43–40 by the All-Star break.

After four years of complaints from both players and fans, Major League Baseball returned to its original single-game format in Cleveland for the 1963 All-Star contest. For the July 9 game played at Municipal Stadium, Henry Aaron started in the outfield, while Warren Spahn and Joe Torre took in the festivities from the bench, as the National League held on for a 5–3 victory.

While the All-Star Game was always considered a celebration of baseball's elite players, off the diamond club executives often used the annual event as an opportunity to schmooze and conduct baseball business. In 1963 Mayor Ivan Allen and his Atlanta contingent used the platform to introduce their city to potential major-league owners. When talks with Charlie Finley of Kansas City stalled, the Atlanta group was desperate for a stadium tenant. Allen quickly arranged a lunch meeting with some of Milwaukee's Rover Boys. By the end of that fateful meeting on July 9, negotiations between Atlanta and the Braves had begun.

Less than two weeks later, the first news linking Atlanta with the Braves leaked. Minutes from the Atlanta Stadium Authority's July 15, 1963, meeting revealed that officials had "discussed briefly the events leading up to an expression of interest in Atlanta by a club other than Kansas City" during their junket in Cleveland. Soon after, sportswriter Bob Broeg predicted in the *St. Louis Post-Dispatch* that if attendance didn't improve in Milwaukee, the Braves would leave for Atlanta. In the first of a series of disconnected denials, team executives did little to dispel the rumors. "We didn't buy the franchise to move to Atlanta," Bartholomay quipped to reporters. "How do these rumors get started?"

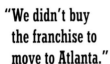

"We didn't buy the franchise to move to Atlanta."
–WILLIAM BARTHOLOMAY

Bill Bartholomay (sitting) and John McHale (standing) (COURTESY OF BOB BUEGE)

Having secured the RBI crown with 130 and connecting for his forty-fourth home run to tie Willie McCovey for the league lead, Henry Aaron almost achieved baseball's triple crown in 1963—but he finished third in the batting race with a .319 average (behind Tommy Davis at .326 and Roberto Clemente at .320). (WHI IMAGE ID 26390)

As Bartholomay continued to deny the rumors in newspapers and on the radio, he spent the next six weeks meeting with various National League owners looking for an answer to the hypothetical question, "If we decided to move the Braves to, say, Atlanta, Georgia, could we count on your vote?"

While their potential franchise move was discussed in boardrooms and baseball executive offices, the Braves flirted with the .500 mark throughout July and August. Warren Spahn continued to rack up career records and ignore any signs he was getting older. On August 13 he not only started his 601st game, breaking Grover Cleveland Alexander's National League record, he also whiffed five Dodgers, raising his career total to 2,383 strikeouts and making him the all-time left-handed strikeout leader. "I think part of what kept that flame burning inside Spahnie was the fact that he felt he had no time to lose," Uecker remembered.

Braves officials sent a confidential memorandum to Atlanta's Stadium Authority on September 4, outlining their interest and requirements to move the Braves to Georgia. Approximately two weeks later a deal in principle was reached to move the team in time for the 1965 season. While a move had not yet been announced publicly, the city of Milwaukee knew the team owners were unhappy, and several prominent Milwaukee businessmen and city officials arranged a private meeting with Bill Bartholomay, John McHale, and Braves executive vice president Tom Reynolds one night in mid-September 1963. As the head of the community group trying to keep the Braves in Milwaukee, influential industrialist Edmund Fitzgerald asked Braves leaders outright, "What do you want? What kind of help can we give you? What will it take to make you happy here in Milwaukee?"

The same day he set the all-time left-handed strikeout record, Warren Spahn filmed a cameo as a German soldier for the television series *Combat!* Spahn had received the Bronze Star and the Purple Heart serving in the U.S. Army during World War II and was the only major-league ballplayer to earn a battlefield commission during the war as a second lieutenant. He later said, "I matured a lot in those three years in the army. . . . If I had not had that maturity, perhaps I never would have pitched until I was almost 45." (DAVID KLUG COLLECTION)

Bartholomay, Reynolds, and McHale played their cards close to their vests, often mentioning the team's poor attendance as a reason for considering relocating the franchise. Carefully avoiding any legal traps by entering into agreements they had no intention of honoring, they discussed the attributes of San Diego and Seattle

ABOVE, LEFT: The "Go to Bat for the Braves" campaign was led by Edmund Fitzgerald (left) and Allan H. "Bud" Selig (right), joined here by Judge Robert Cannon (far left) and Eddie Mathews. (MILWAUKEE JOURNAL SENTINEL)

ABOVE, RIGHT: The Braves' future looked promising in 1963 with an influx of young arms including Wade Blasingame, Denny Lemaster, Hank Fischer, Bob Sadowski, and Tony Cloninger. (DAVID KLUG COLLECTION)

BELOW, LEFT: To generate interest in season tickets, Johnny Logan, Denis Menke, Bobby Bragan, Henry Aaron, Edmund Fitzgerald, Del Crandall, and John McHale participated in numerous "Go to Bat for the Braves" luncheons during the off-season. (MILWAUKEE JOURNAL SENTINEL)

BELOW, RIGHT: Bill Bartholomay criticized Milwaukee's "baseball climate," despite the Braves outdrawing the Cubs during ten of the previous twelve seasons and averaging 94.4 tickets sold per 100 residents each year, compared to an average of 22.2 for other National League cities and 20.7 for American League cities over the same period. (NATIONAL BASEBALL HALL OF FAME LIBRARY)

> **"We were going out to dinners and making appearances and eating a lot of chicken pot pie, but about all we were getting out of it was a bellyful of chicken pot pie."**
>
> —TOM REYNOLDS

as possible suitors for the team, but they never mentioned Atlanta. Hoping to appease the disgruntled owners, Fitzgerald's group agreed to spearhead a "Go to Bat for the Braves" campaign to help boost season ticket sales to 7,500 seats and secure a $550,000 deal for radio and television rights—amounts established by Bartholomay, McHale, and Reynolds. With that, the Rover Boys had acquired the leverage they needed to finalize negotiations with Atlanta.

Meanwhile, Bobby Bragan's first year with the Braves found the team finishing with an 84–78 record and a .519 winning percentage, their worst since moving to Milwaukee. Losing thirty-one games by one run, the Braves slipped into sixth place in the ten-team league. "Pitching was our downfall," Bragan claimed. "But I was firmly convinced [Denny] Lemaster and [Tony] Cloninger were the key to Milwaukee's future, a potential lefty-righty combination to replace Spahn-Burdette. One more good season from Spahnie and then the kids would be able to carry the pitching load themselves."

Only 773,018 fans visited County Stadium in 1963, and rumors of the team's exodus intensified. The whispers were so persistent that John McHale issued a cryptic statement: "The Braves will be in Milwaukee, today, tomorrow, next year and as long as we are welcome." Still, after the "Go to Bat for the Braves" campaign sold fewer than four thousand advance season tickets, the Braves' owners concluded that the city was no longer interested in reinvigorating the franchise. "When we began to look around and inquire about results in late January," Tom Reynolds recounted to Furman Bisher in *Miracle in Atlanta: The Atlanta Braves Story*, "we got a lot of blank stares. We were going out to dinners and making appearances and eating a lot of chicken pot pie, but about all we were getting out of it was a bellyful of chicken pot pie. We weren't getting any results. In short, these people, for all their good intentions and promises, were falling flat on their faces."

Even more discouraging, the "Go to Bat for the Braves" committee secured only a $400,000 offer for the Braves' broadcast rights for the upcoming season, well short of their $550,000 goal. In the current offer, from the Schlitz Brewing Company, it almost felt like television rights were thrown in for good measure, since for radio alone the offer had been $375,000 the two previous years. On the heels of the failed "Go to Bat for the Braves" campaign, Braves executives reconnected with Atlanta's officials.

Meeting at the O'Hare Inn in early February, Bartholomay and the Braves promised to play in Atlanta if a major-league-caliber stadium was available to host them for the 1965 season. Although the men walked out of the meeting with a twenty-five-year contract between the Braves and the city, no press conference was called or media release drafted. Instead, with the deal in hand, Atlanta mayor Ivan Allen Jr. leaked a story to the *Atlanta Constitution* on March 5 insinuating that an unnamed major-league franchise had committed to relocating to Georgia in 1965 if a stadium could be built in time. The next day Atlanta officials approved funding for an $18 million

This left Bragan in the precarious position of trying to manage the rookie left fielder's personality while getting him to produce in the everyday lineup. "[Rico] didn't take things as seriously as he should have. But he was so temperamental and so talented, Bragan had to either take it a little easier on him or run him off, and the team was better off with Rico than without him," said future Braves pitcher Billy O'Dell.

But the infusion of Carty's power couldn't compensate for the team's depleted pitching staff. Although Denny Lemaster posted a respectable 8–6 record through the Fourth of July, Tony Cloninger was stuck at 7–7, Bob Sadowski floundered at 3–6, and Warren Spahn had to endure a 5–8 record. By the All-Star break the Braves' 38–40 record already had them ten and a half games behind the first-place Philadelphia Phillies. "The National League was turning over in those years," Henry Aaron explained, "and it was turning over on the Braves. We didn't have the speed that the Dodgers and Cardinals had, and when Spahn finally lost it, we couldn't match Koufax or [Bob] Gibson [of the St. Louis Cardinals]."

When baseball's elite gathered at New York's Shea Stadium on July 7 for the 1964 All-Star Game, a recent article in *The Sporting News* had sportswriters and baseball officials chattering among themselves on elevators, in press quarters, and in smoke-filled rooms. The story, attributed to an "unimpeachable source," claimed that the Braves planned to move to Atlanta in 1965, and the national media ran with the revelation. The Braves' All-Star representatives, Henry Aaron and starting catcher Joe Torre, were hounded by the press. In an attempt to lighten the situation, Torre hammed it up the day of the game by pasting a felt "A" onto his baseball cap. Even after the National League pulled out an exciting ninth-inning rally for a 7–4 victory, it seemed the only thing the national media could focus on was the franchise that was about to abandon Milwaukee. "For me this was a lot different than the move from Boston," Eddie Mathews said. "I never had any roots in Boston, and most of us were young guys then. Now my family lived in the Milwaukee area. I liked Atlanta, and I had friends there, but I sure as hell didn't want to move there."

Following the All-Star Game, *The Sporting News* and the *New York Times* confirmed that the Braves would play the next year in Atlanta. Team officials continued to issue murky denials. "This rumor . . . has gone full circle," John McHale waffled to reporters all season long. "How many times do we have to keep answering?"

Despite the drama unfolding in the newspapers, the Braves began to turn their season around. Winning sixteen of twenty-four games through the first of August, they shortened their deficit behind the first-place Phillies to six and a half games. By late August, Cloninger and Lemaster were having fine seasons—Cloninger ended up winning nineteen games, and Lemaster got seventeen victories—but the rest of the Braves starters had the habit of giving up one more run than the team could score.

> "I liked Atlanta, and I had friends there, but I sure as hell didn't want to move there."
>
> —EDDIE MATHEWS

In the clubhouse, morale stayed strong despite the possibility of the team relocating. "In 1964 we still had that great camaraderie, and the reason was we were still a winning ball club, still in contention all the time," Lemaster remembered. "And in that season Spahn and Bragan were always in each other's face."

Although he had signed an $85,000 contract prior to the 1964 season, making him the highest-paid pitcher in baseball, Warren Spahn had finally started giving in to age. The southpaw's ERA had more than doubled from the previous year, and after his nearly five thousand innings of work in the big leagues, Bragan dropped him from the starting rotation. "We should have been expecting it," Aaron admitted. "He finally hit the wall in 1964. He still looked like himself, with the fancy windup and the big leg kick, but there was nothing left on the ball."

Looking for a graceful way to transition the veteran out of uniform, Bragan demoted a disgruntled Spahn to the bullpen. "During the '64 season my relationship with Warren Spahn completely soured," Bragan wrote. "There was no question why we weren't getting along."

Spahn was determined to continue pitching, regardless of Bragan's reassignment. "If an athlete's ego won't let him accept the fact that it's time to retire, that's where the problem comes in," Mathews wrote. "Spahnie pitched a few more good games, but mostly he got hit hard. It hurt me—it hurt all of his teammates—to watch him getting knocked around like that. He deserved a better finish."

Returning to the starting rotation for a couple of late-season starts with little success, Spahn failed to win more games than he lost for the first time since 1952, finishing with a 6–13 record. "The sad part about it was that we might have won the pennant in 1964 if he'd been even a shadow of the old Spahn," Aaron speculated. But time had finally caught up to Spahn. In November, the future Hall of Famer was granted his wish to pitch elsewhere and was sold to the Mets. "Spahn had every chance to stay with the Braves, first as one of the team radio broadcasters, then as a roving pitching coach," Aaron recalled. "I think the Braves were fair with Spahn. I think he blew it himself. His record the next season with the Giants and Mets proved the Braves were right."

But before Spahn turned in his Milwaukee flannels, the Braves finished their 1964 season at County Stadium against the Pirates. "For the last game of the year, Bragan decided it would be a clever idea to have me manage the team while he sat in the stands and watched," veteran third baseman Mathews recalled. The unique

Behind center fielder Lee Maye (sliding into third base), who led the senior circuit in doubles, Milwaukee in 1964 featured five players with twenty or more home runs and led the National League in runs, doubles, on-base percentage, and slugging percentage, while their batting average of .272 was tied for the league's best. (DAVID KLUG COLLECTION)

After amassing 356 career victories, 2,493 strikeouts, and 5,046 innings during 714 pitching appearances for the Braves, Warren Spahn was sold to the New York Mets on November 23, 1964. (ROBERT KOEHLER COLLECTION)

situation provided Mathews not only his first taste of being a major-league skipper but also an opportunity to take advantage of the magnitude of the situation: "For all we knew, this was going to be the Braves' final game in Milwaukee. We were winning going into the ninth inning, 6–0. I decided to put Hank and myself into the game for the last inning, along with a few other veterans, just to give the fans one last chance to see us. I also took out the pitcher, Bob Sadowski, even though he was pitching a shutout, and put in Warren Spahn to finish the game. He hadn't won a game in three months, but if we were leaving, who else would you want as the last Braves pitcher? The fans gave him a huge ovation."

The Braves' 6–0 victory over the Pirates was bittersweet, the culmination of a September streak that saw the team gain nine games on first place. The Braves finished the season with an 88–74 record. "We didn't really start to play ball until the last couple weeks of the season. We won 13 of our last 15 games and made up a lot of ground, but the best we could do was finish five games back," Mathews said regretfully.

Although the Braves never seriously contended for the pennant in 1964, attendance at County Stadium increased slightly to 910,911. But only 36,000 Milwaukeeans attended the final six home games, one more sign that fans were disgusted with the team's continued denials of a relocation to Atlanta.

As the season wound down, Bartholomay continued to dismiss the rumors publicly but privately avoided committing to any sort of a future in Milwaukee. When Milwaukee County officials offered to renegotiate the Braves' stadium lease—suggesting an annual rent of one dollar up to the first million admissions, along with a new deal on concessions and maintenance that would save the Braves an additional $120,000 a year—the Braves' owners declined, claiming to be fully satisfied with their existing lease. In September Schlitz Brewing Company offered a three-year broadcast sponsorship deal that represented a 33 percent increase over the team's existing contract; Bartholomay also turned it down. Just ten days after telling the press that it would be a personal disappointment to leave Milwaukee, Bartholomay scheduled a press conference.

Following a meeting of National League officials and club owners to discuss plans for the Braves' transfer from Milwaukee to Atlanta, National League president Warren Giles was flanked by John McHale (left) and Bill Bartholomay (right) during a press conference. (DAVID KLUG COLLECTION)

On the afternoon of October 21, 1964, an army of television and radio press anxiously waited inside an improvised pressroom at Chicago's Ambassador East Hotel. At 1:50 p.m., Milwaukee Braves publicity director and former relief pitcher Ernie Johnson entered the room with a press release in hand and confirmed the rumors: "The board of directors of the Milwaukee Braves, Inc., voted today to request the permission of the National League to transfer their franchise to Atlanta, Georgia, for 1965."

The same Braves franchise that in 1953 had become the first club in fifty years to relocate would become the first club to switch cities twice. And for the first time, a city was about to be stripped altogether of its major-league status. While the forsaken fans of the Boston Braves, St. Louis Browns, Brooklyn Dodgers, New York Giants, and Washington Senators had lost teams to relocation, they had the option to transfer their allegiances to the other major-league team across town. The Milwaukee fans immediately lashed out at the Braves' owners not only for their desertion but also for their conscious deception. Their anger was summarized in a third-grader's crayoned note sent to Bartholomay that proclaimed: "YOU ARE A LIAR."

Milwaukee still had a legal trump card to play, because the Braves' stadium lease ran through 1965. After paying $200,000 in rent during the 1964 season, Bartholomay assumed that the county would accept a $500,000 cash settlement to buy out the contract's final year. Instead, the county board voted unanimously to reject the offer and authorized counsel to incur any expense necessary to keep the Braves in town. Accusing the Braves of antitrust violations, Milwaukee County filed suit. "Milwaukee politicians who hadn't seen the Braves in years suddenly became devout fans," Donald Davidson remembered in *Caught Short*. "Bartholomay, John McHale, part owner and general manager, and the other owners were unjustly and hostilely accused of being

After Milwaukee's tumultuous 1964 season, Braves pitcher and Oshkosh, Wisconsin, native Billy Hoeft claimed to a reporter that manager Bobby Bragan tried to lose games by regularly switching around the team's lineup. (ALL-AMERICAN SPORTS, LLC)

money-minded carpetbaggers." The animosity grew so heated that public officials claimed the team had sabotaged the season to make the city look bad. According to Davidson, "Eugene Grobschmidt, outspoken chairman of the Milwaukee County Board, actually accused Bragan and the Braves of purposely losing games," citing Bragan's 110 different starting lineups as proof.

Grobschmidt convinced board members to call for an investigation of Braves management's possible contract violations in ticket sales practices and "apparent

(From left to right) Milwaukee County Board chairman Eugene Grobschmidt, county executive John Doyne, and *Milwaukee Sentinel* sports editor Lloyd Larsen held a press conference at General Mitchell Field upon returning from a meeting with National League owners. (MILWAUKEE JOURNAL SENTINEL)

ineptitude." The County Board further reasoned that a championship would have made it impossible to justify the Braves' departure for Atlanta. "That, of course, was ridiculous," Eddie Mathews said. "Despite what Bragan's ego seemed to believe, it was the ballplayers, not the manager, who won or lost games. Bragan did his thing, right or wrong, but there's no way he was ever trying to lose. Absolutely not. He's not that kind of person. He could be very sarcastic, and quite honestly I didn't think he was a good manager, but as far as losing on purpose—no way in hell."

Undaunted by the pending lawsuit and proposed inquiry, team officials began transferring operations to rented offices in Atlanta during the off-season. About two weeks after the Braves' owners officially announced their intentions, the National League gave the team permission to move to Atlanta, but not until 1966. That left Milwaukee with one last, sad summer to either save their Braves franchise or prepare to be the first city abandoned by big-league sports. "For the players—and the fans—it was horrible to see our team and our city going at each other in court, like a messy, bitter divorce," Henry Aaron remembered. "We loved Milwaukee, and none of us wanted to move, but it was hard for us to tell the good guys from the bad guys."

In a cartoon entitled "But your honor, I don't want a divorce," artist Al Rainovic captured the feelings of many Milwaukee fans who were coming to terms with the Braves' relocation south. (UWM LIBRARIES, ARCHIVES DEPARTMENT RAINOVIC COLLECTION IMAGE 250)

THE
Departure
1965

Milwaukee's once-hot romance with the Braves had deteriorated into a full-fledged, mud-flinging divorce. Before the start of the 1965 season, the county continued to refuse owner Bill Bartholomay's $500,000 buyout offer unless the National League promised to replace the Braves with an expansion franchise. Showing their contempt for the team's lame-duck status, the Braves' owners removed "Milwaukee" from all team-licensed souvenirs and merchandise. At souvenir stands around County Stadium, baseball caps with the "M" were replaced with ones sporting a block-letter "A." Magazine-sized scorecards became nothing more than a couple of pages wrapped around a roster insert. The team's yearbook was shrunk to half its previous size, made no mention of Milwaukee on the cover, and listed the Braves franchise's address in Atlanta. Claiming that the club had lost $3.5 million in Milwaukee, due in large part to flagging attendance, the owners blamed the "anti-baseball climate" for driving them away. "The team and ownership were continually being knocked down, besmirched and vilified," president and general manager John McHale claimed the following year. "Taking a crack at the Braves became a political pastime in Milwaukee, which, together with the unfriendly press, set the stage for killing baseball."

While referring publicly to the community's alleged hostility as their excuse for leaving, Bartholomay and his associates' actions reminded fans across the country that the national pastime was, after all, a business—one motivated by the almighty dollar. Because baseball didn't pool local television and radio broadcast revenues to distribute equally among the teams, owners were free to squeeze their individual domains dry without sharing a drop with fellow owners. Although selling broadcast rights was not yet a billion-dollar revenue stream, it was fast becoming a lucrative

As County Stadium's final night of hosting the Braves began, first baseman Gene Oliver stood for the final rendition of the National Anthem. (COURTESY OF BOB BUEGE)

Bill Bartholomay show-cased Atlanta's soon-to-be-completed stadium as the future home of the Braves. (DAVID KLUG COLLECTION)

> "Taking a crack at the Braves became a political pastime in Milwaukee."
>
> —JOHN MCHALE

source of income. In 1964 the Milwaukee Braves received $400,000 for their local broadcasts, slightly below league average. At season's end, the Schlitz Brewing Company offered the Braves $535,000 a year for three years, but Milwaukee's limited advertising market of 2.5 million television households halted at Chicago to the south, Minneapolis to the west, Canada to the north, and Lake Michigan to the east. Atlanta offered a seven-state empire of six million baseball-deprived households between the Atlantic Ocean and the Mississippi River. The team received $2.5 million from Coca-Cola for its first broadcast contract in Atlanta, as Braves ownership cashed in on Major League Baseball's neglect of the South.

Milwaukee fans soon turned their passion for the Braves into an exercise of spite. "City stores and banks removed Braves schedules from their counters. Because Atlanta was the home city of the Coca-Cola Company, Milwaukee bars and restaurants stopped selling Coke," manager Bobby Bragan recalled. "It was horrible."

Back in 1953, Milwaukee could not have predicted the consequences of demonstrating to baseball owners how profitable moving a franchise could be. Now Atlanta had followed Milwaukee's formula for seducing a willing franchise with the enticement of a new, teamless stadium and the opportunity to rebrand a community as Big League. "If ever a city lifted its skirts and crooked its finger and winked its eye at a susceptible, fan-rejected, unloved baseball franchise," proclaimed Furman Bisher in *Miracle in Atlanta: The Atlanta Braves Story*, "Milwaukee is the guilty party."

During the off-season, the Braves made no attempt to market tickets in Milwaukee; after selling 4,477 season tickets for the 1964 season, they had sold only 36 before opening day of 1965. By mid-February team officials were desperate to boost ticket sales and generate any sort of revenue. They approached the same group of local Milwaukee businessmen whose "Go to Bat for the Braves" campaign had fallen short, with an offer to put ticket sales proceeds in a fund to help promote and preserve big-league baseball in Milwaukee.

The club offered five cents per ticket on the first 766,927 tickets sold—a figure chosen to match the Braves' previous low attendance in Milwaukee, then twenty-five cents per ticket between that number and one million, and a dollar per ticket for each ticket over the million mark. The group was now formally organized as Teams, Inc., and was led by the twenty-nine-year-old son of Wisconsin's biggest Ford dealer, Allan "Bud" Selig, and Edmund Fitzgerald, president of Cutler-Hammer Company. Teams, Inc., used the opportunity to reassure major-league owners that Milwaukee was still a major-league-caliber city by organizing the "Stand Up for Milwaukee Day" ticket drive for County Stadium's Opening Day and attracted 33,874 fans. Embarrassed

Gary Manteufel and Paul Dankert proved that there was often plenty of space around County Stadium before games in 1965 to get in a game of catch. (MILWAUKEE JOURNAL SENTINEL)

field for his 394th career home run. But as Aaron circled the bases, plate umpire Chris Pelekoudas called him out for stepping outside of the batter's box. "Well, just about our entire ballclub went nuts. Pelekoudas wound up ejecting several of our guys," Torre recalled. "If he hadn't, the magical number atop the all-time home-run list would be 756, not 755." The Braves played the remainder of the game under protest, until Tony Cloninger held on for the 5–3 win and his eighteenth victory of the season.

The win, combined with a Dodgers loss, put Milwaukee in first place after April for the first time since 1959. But the Braves proceeded to drop nine of their next eleven games, including six in a row at County Stadium. Their swift descent in the standings prompted Milwaukee County Board chairman Eugene Grobschmidt to once again question the team's motives, implying that they didn't act like a team that wanted to win and saying, "[I]t would look silly if they played the World Series here and then moved to Atlanta."

The thirteen-year union between Milwaukee and the Braves was damaged beyond repair. Team management began hurling insults back at the politicians. "Bragan told the press that Milwaukee would still own the Braves if the county had been as interested in not losing the team as politicians now were in the team's losing games," Donald Davidson recalled.

On the field, Bragan piloted a brief pitching renaissance in September that got the Braves within two and a half games of first place. "In New York on September 10 through 12, Braves hurlers pitched back-to-back one-hitters, then lost a heartbreaking 1–0, ten-inning game that signaled the beginning of the end for pennant aspirations," Braves historian Bob Buege wrote.

The Braves' pennant drive finally fizzled as they dropped fourteen of their final twenty-one games. Their late-season efforts featured a potent offense that built leads with the bats of Henry Aaron, Eddie Mathews, Mack Jones, Joe Torre, Felipe Alou, and Gene Oliver, but the pitching staff couldn't hold those leads. "We were a club that could pound the ball as well as anyone," Torre said of the 1965 team that set a National League record with six players hitting at least twenty home runs—and finished fifth. "Our problem was that we couldn't hold down the other teams. We

Milwaukee's sluggers led the National League in home runs with 196 as a record six players—(from left to right) Felipe Alou, Henry Aaron, Gene Oliver, Eddie Mathews, and (not pictured) Mack Jones and Joe Torre—all hit at least twenty homers. (ROBERT KOEHLER COLLECTION)

As the end of the 1965 season neared, the Braves shared their County Stadium clubhouse with Vince Lombardi's Green Bay Packers. (ROBERT KOEHLER COLLECTION)

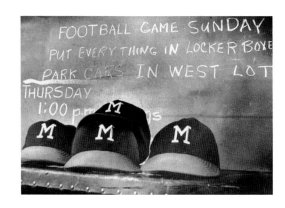

never had enough pitching. I joined the Braves just as the golden years of pitchers—Spahn, Burdette and Buhl—were running out. The pitchers who followed them, such as Tony Cloninger, Hank Fischer, Wade Blasingame, and Denny Lemaster, never developed into the same kind of consistent winners."

Playing their final ten games on the road in San Francisco, Houston, and Los Angeles, the Braves finished eleven games behind the pennant-winning Dodgers with an 86–76 record. As Joe Torre explained, "We were never terrible but almost always barely a notch above mediocre." County Stadium attendance reached an all-time low of 555,584 for the year. Having lost three out of four fans who had followed the Braves during the late '50s, the stadium's income didn't even begin to cover costs, and the team lost nearly $1 million while playing out a season that no one wanted.

As the 1965 season wound down, the majority of Milwaukee's baseball headlines came from the courtroom. Beginning on August 6 Wisconsin attorney general Bronson La Follette waged an attack on organized baseball and filed antitrust lawsuits against the Braves and the

The Braves' 1965 pitching staff was led by Tony Cloninger, who won a Milwaukee-era record twenty-four games. (ALL-AMERICAN SPORTS, LLC)

> **"We were never terrible but almost always barely a notch above mediocre."**
>
> —JOE TORRE

National League. The suits charged that by approving the Braves' transfer without providing Milwaukee a replacement team, the National League conspired to restrain trade and damage the state's economy. Rather than sue in federal court, where baseball's well-established antitrust exemption would prevail, the grandson of famous U.S. Senator Robert M. La Follette filed the action in state court under Wisconsin's antitrust law. If victorious, the state could seek injunctions in other states forbidding teams to play Braves home games anywhere but in Milwaukee. A win would set a precedent for other states to bring similar suits against Major League Baseball and force them to grant franchises to their cities or else pay damages.

Never before had Major League Baseball faced a state-level antitrust challenge. Legal experts recognized that baseball's federal exemption might be undone by an adverse ruling that other states would have to respect under the U.S. Constitution's "full faith and credit" clause. It could end the nation's only federally protected legal monopoly, dating back to 1922—what legal scholars termed "the baseball anomaly." The National League scrambled to defend itself. Baseball retained veteran antitrust attorney and future baseball commissioner Bowie Kuhn, who later confessed that moving the Braves "gave baseball an irresponsible, gypsy look."

In open court, state's attorneys offered to drop the suit in exchange for a new franchise. But the owners protested, claiming that Wisconsin was holding the National League hostage until it promised Milwaukee an expansion team. In its trial brief of November 1965, the state asserted that "Milwaukee is an excellent baseball town, that it is a disgrace to all baseball that it no longer has a major league team, that baseball is a monopoly, and that if it can't behave better than it has, it deserves to be regulated."

The ensuing trial in Judge Elmer Roller's Milwaukee courtroom had lifted the veil of innocence from the national pastime to expose the sport's true visage—one of greed-motivated monopoly. "There were so many appeals and rulings, restraining orders and injunctions, charges and counter-charges, depositions and whereases, hereuntos and therefores that the general public was lost in the maze," Furman Bisher wrote in *Miracle in Atlanta*. "It was becoming a battle royal with any and all combatants invited, but you had to bring your own brass knuckles."

ABOVE, LEFT: By challenging baseball's long-standing antitrust exemption, Wisconsin attorney general Bronson La Follette (center, with glasses) and special counsel for Milwaukee County Steven E. Keane (seated on desk with hands folded) looked to prevent the Braves' move to Atlanta. (MILWAUKEE JOURNAL SENTINEL)

ABOVE, RIGHT: In Judge Elmer Roller's courtroom, special counsel for the state of Wisconsin Willard Stafford (second from left) faced off against Braves attorney Ray McCann (just right of court clerk in center) and Major League Baseball's counselor Bowie Kuhn (far right). (MILWAUKEE JOURNAL SENTINEL)

BELOW: Some optimistic Braves fans still hoped the team would return to Milwaukee following the 1965 season. (MILWAUKEE JOURNAL SENTINEL)

While the battle for the Braves continued in the courtroom that winter, the team decided to move to Atlanta and let Milwaukee's lawsuit run its course. With their fate still undecided, the Braves finished spring training and headed to Atlanta for Opening Day. Arriving to a welcoming parade in Atlanta similar to the one in Milwaukee thirteen years earlier, the Braves were determined to host their home opener at Atlanta Stadium against the Pittsburgh Pirates. Owner Bill Bartholomay defiantly proclaimed, "There is as much chance of the Braves playing in Milwaukee this summer as there is of the New York Yankees."

With the team's fate in the hands of the court, Milwaukee had prepared County Stadium on April 12 for the 1966 season's home opener in the event of a decision to return the team to Wisconsin. The next day, Judge Roller ruled against the National League, claiming the Braves franchise had violated Wisconsin's antitrust laws. The ruling stated that if the National League couldn't find Milwaukee a new baseball team by 1967, they'd have to return the Braves to Milwaukee within one month. The National League appealed to the state's Supreme Court and won later that summer. Following a series of injunctions, rulings, reversals, and appeals that continued throughout the 1966 season and into the winter, the state of Wisconsin asked that the U.S. Supreme Court hear the case. On December 12, 1966, the high court voted 4–3 to refuse to hear the final appeal and took no action, upholding baseball's exemption from antitrust laws and ending the Braves' legal brawl. Atlanta finally had its Braves.

For twelve years in Milwaukee, Eddie Mathews and Henry Aaron terrorized National League pitchers, averaging nearly seventy-one homers and 215 runs batted in per season. (COURTESY OF BOB BUEGE)

◆ ◆ ◆

Back on September 22, 1965, while the war waged on in the courtroom, the Braves hosted the Dodgers on a somber Wednesday evening. "The 12,577 mourners who attended the graveside ceremony did not wear black arm bands or veils, but they may as well have," Bob Buege recalled in *The Milwaukee Braves: A Baseball Eulogy*. "On a pleasant evening in early autumn of 1965, the remains of the Milwaukee Braves Baseball Club were finally laid to rest in ground formerly occupied by the Old Soldiers' Home."

On the mound for the pennant-bound Dodgers that night was Sandy Koufax, who was about to win the second of his three Cy Young Awards, while Milwaukee countered with its southpaw ace, Wade Blasingame. But on that night Koufax couldn't handle the Braves, and he gave up five runs and was pulled by the third inning. Milwaukee built a commanding 6–1 lead behind a Frank Bolling grand slam, a solo homer by Mack Jones, and an inside-the-park homer from Gene Oliver. But the Dodgers battled back to cut the lead to 6–3 in the fourth, and before the fifth inning ended it was tied at 6.

> **"It was the end of an era and the end of probably the best years of my life."**
> —EDDIE MATHEWS

As the game went into the late innings, County Stadium fans put aside their bitterness toward the Braves' owners and expressed their gratitude toward the players. "As you might expect, that was a very emotional night," Eddie Mathews confessed. "The reality of leaving Milwaukee was sinking in. Most of the ballplayers didn't want to go to Atlanta. Aaron and I had been around the longest, and we certainly didn't want to go. The fans cheered us all night, but when I came to bat in the last of the eighth, for what looked like the last time in Milwaukee, the fans gave me about a two-minute standing ovation. I was overwhelmed. My eyes filled up with tears. I tried to bat, but I had to step out of the batter's box three or four times. I know I finally did bat. I don't remember it, though. Everything was a blur. I felt very humble at that moment. Everyone should have a moment like that in his life."

With the score still tied at 6, the game went into extra innings. The Dodgers finally pulled ahead in the eleventh when Maury Wills bunted for a hit, stole second, and scored on a single. In the Braves' half of the inning, Mack Jones beat out an infield single and represented the tying run. With one out, Aaron stepped to the plate but lined out to center field. Jones was abruptly doubled off first. "When the game ended and we lost, 7–6, the whole crowd stood and gave us the longest ovation on record. Many of us came out of the dugout and kind of doffed our hats to those wonderful folks. It was the end of an era and the end of probably the best years of my life," Mathews admitted.

The Braves' 1,016th and final game at County Stadium ended in extra innings, just like their first back in 1953. When the team's era in Wisconsin ended, they had never

After years of blaring "Charge" at County Stadium, trumpeter Dick Emmons was often heard reciting "Taps" during the Braves' final few innings in Milwaukee. (DAVID KLUG COLLECTION)

finished lower than six games over .500, placed second five times, and won the pennant twice as the only major-league club never to suffer a losing season while in one city. It was poetic that on the Braves' last night in Milwaukee, the only two players remaining from the 1957 world championship walked together up the long, cold cement County Stadium corridor. Once Henry Aaron and Eddie Mathews disappeared behind the Braves' clubhouse door, the end of an era was at hand. The team that had made Milwaukee famous was gone forever.

MILWAUKEE BRAVES
ALL-TIME ROSTER: 1953–1965

PLAYERS

Aaron, Henry	1954–65	Carty, Rico	1963–65
Aaron, Tommie	1962–63, 1965	Chrisley, Neil	1961
Adcock, Joe	1953–62	Cimoli, Gino	1961
Alomar, Sandy	1964–65	Cline, Ty	1963–65
Alou, Felipe	1964–65	Cloninger, Tony	1961–65
Antonelli, Johnny	1953	Cole, Dave	1953
Aspromonte, Ken	1962	Cole, Dick	1957
Atwell, Toby	1956	Conley, Gene	1954–58
Avila, Bobby	1959	Constable, Jim	1962
Bailey, Ed	1964	Cooper, Walker	1953
Beauchamp, Jim	1965	Cottier, Chuck	1959–60
Bedell, Howie	1962	Covington, Wes	1956–61
Bell, Gus	1962–64	Cowan, Billy	1965
Bickford, Vern	1953	Crandall, Del	1953–63
Blackaby, Ethan	1962, 1964	Crone, Ray	1954–57
Blanchard, Johnny	1965	Crowe, George	1953, 1955
Blasingame, Wade	1963–65	Curtis, Jack	1962
Bolling, Frank	1961–65	Dark, Alvin	1960
Boone, Ray	1959–60	de la Hoz, Mike	1964–65
Boyd, Bob	1961	DeMerit, John	1957–59, 1961
Braun, John	1964	Dillard, Don	1963, 1965
Brunet, George	1960–61	Dittmer, Jack	1953–56
Bruton, Bill	1953–60	Drabowsky, Moe	1961
Buhl, Bob	1953–62	Edelman, John	1955
Burdette, Lou	1953–63	Eilers, Dave	1964–65
Burris, Paul	1953	Fischer, Hank	1962–65
Butler, Cecil	1962, 1964	Fox, Terry	1960
Calderone, Sam	1954	Funk, Frank	1963
Carroll, Clay	1964–65	Gabrielson, Len	1960, 1963–64

Giggie, Bob	1959–60	Maye, Lee	1959–65
Gonder, Jesse	1965	McMahon, Don	1957–62
Gordon, Sid	1953	McMillan, Roy	1961–64
Gorin, Charlie	1954–55	Menke, Denis	1962–65
Haas, Eddie	1958, 1960	Metkovich, George	1954
Hanebrink, Harry	1953, 1957–58	Morehead, Seth	1961
Hartman, Bob	1959	Morgan, Joe	1959
Hazle, Bob	1957–58	Morton, Bubba	1963
Hendley, Bob	1961–63	Murff, Red	1956–57
Hersh, Earl	1956	Nichols, Chet	1954–56
Hoeft, Billy	1964	Niekro, Phil	1964–65
Jay, Joey	1953–55, 1957–60	Nottebart, Don	1960–62
Jester, Virgil	1953	O'Brien, Johnny	1959
Johnson, Ernie	1953–58	O'Connell, Danny	1954–57
Johnson, Ken	1965	O'Dell, Billy	1965
Johnson, Lou	1962	Oliver, Gene	1963–65
Jolly, Dave	1953–57	Olivo, Chi-Chi	1961, 1964–65
Jones, Mack	1961–63, 1965	Osinski, Dan	1965
Jones, Nippy	1957	Pafko, Andy	1953–59
Kelley, Dick	1964–65	Paine, Phil	1954–57
Klaus, Billy	1953	Pendleton, Jim	1953–56
Klimchock, Lou	1962, 1963–65	Phillips, Taylor	1956–57
Kolb, Gary	1964–65	Piche, Ron	1960–63
Koppe, Joe	1958	Pisoni, Jim	1959
Koslo, Dave	1954–55	Pizarro, Juan	1957–60
Krsnich, Mike	1960, 1962	Queen, Billy	1954
Larker, Norm	1963	Ranew, Merritt	1964
Lary, Frank	1964	Raymond, Claude	1961–63
Lau, Charlie	1960–61	Rice, Del	1955–59
Lemaster, Denny	1962–65	Roach, Mel	1953–54, 1957–61
Liddle, Don	1953	Robinson, Humberto	1955–56, 1958
Littlefield, Dick	1958	Roof, Phil	1961, 1964
Logan, Johnny	1953–61	Roselli, Bob	1955–56, 1958
Lopata, Stan	1959–60	Rush, Bob	1958–60
Mackenzie, Ken	1960–61	Sadowski, Bob	1963–65
Malkmus, Bobby	1957	Samuel, Amado	1962–63
Mantilla, Felix	1956–61	Sawatski, Carl	1957–58
Martin, Billy	1961	Schneider, Dan	1963–64
Mathews, Eddie	1953–65	Schoendienst, Red	1957–60

Shaw, Bob	1962–63
Shearer, Ray	1957
Sisti, Sibby	1953–54
Slaughter, Enos	1959
Sleater, Lou	1956
Smalley, Roy	1954
Smith, Jack	1964
Southworth, Bill	1964
Spahn, Warren	1953–64
Spangler, Al	1959–61
St. Claire, Ebba	1953
Surkont, Max	1953
Tanner, Chuck	1955–57
Taylor, Ben	1955
Taylor, Hawk	1957–58, 1961–63
Thomas, Frank	1961, 1965
Thomson, Bobby	1954–57
Thorpe, Bob	1953
Tiefenauer, Bobby	1963–65
Torre, Frank	1956–60
Torre, Joe	1960–65
Trowbridge, Bob	1956–59
Uecker, Bob	1962–63
Umbach, Arnold	1964
Vargas, Roberto	1955
Vernon, Mickey	1959
White, Charlie	1954–55
White, Sammy	1961
Willey, Carlton	1958–62
Wilson, Jim	1953–54
Wise, Casey	1958–59
Woodward, Woody	1963–65

MANAGERS

Bragan, Bobby	1963–65
Dressen, Charlie	1960–61
Grimm, Charlie	1953–56
Haney, Fred	1956–59
Tebbetts, Birdie	1961–62

COACHES

Adair, Bill	1962
Cooney, John	1953–55
Dykes, Jimmy	1962
Fitzpatrick, John	1958–59
Haney, Fred	1956
Herman, Billy	1958–59
Keely, Bob	1953–57
Myatt, George	1960–61
Pafko, Andy	1960–62
Riddle, John	1957
Root, Charlie	1956–57
Ryan, Connie	1957
Scheffing, Bob	1960
Silvestri, Ken	1963–65
Walker, Dixie	1963–65
Walters, Bucky	1953–55
White, Jo Jo	1963–65
Wyatt, Whitlow	1958–65

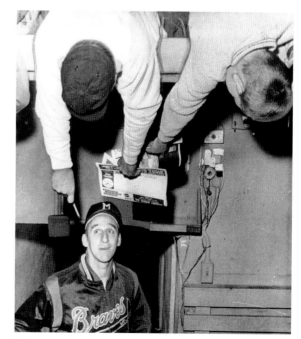

Warren Spahn had one of baseball's most recognizable faces. (DAVID KLUG COLLECTION)

MILWAUKEE BRAVES ON THE NATIONAL LEAGUE ALL-STAR TEAM ROSTER

1953
Crandall, Del
Mathews, Eddie
Spahn, Warren

1954
Conley, Gene
Crandall, Del
Spahn, Warren
Wilson, Jim

1955
Aaron, Henry
Conley, Gene
Crandall, Del
Logan, Johnny
Mathews, Eddie

1956
Aaron, Henry
Crandall, Del
Mathews, Eddie
Spahn, Warren

1957
Aaron, Henry
Burdette, Lou
Logan, Johnny
Mathews, Eddie
Schoendienst, Red
Spahn, Warren

1958
Aaron, Henry
Crandall, Del
Logan, Johnny
Mathews, Eddie
McMahon, Don
Spahn, Waren

1959
Aaron, Henry
Burdette, Lou
Crandall, Del
Logan, Johnny
 (second game only)
Mathews, Eddie
Spahn, Warren

1960
Aaron, Henry
Adcock, Joe
Buhl, Bob
Crandall, Del
Mathews, Eddie

1961
Aaron, Henry
Bolling, Frank
Mathews, Eddie
Spahn, Warren

1962
Aaron, Henry
Bolling, Frank
Crandall, Del
Mathews, Eddie
Shaw, Bob
Spahn, Warren

1963
Aaron, Henry
Spahn, Warren
Torre, Joe

1964
Aaron, Henry
Torre, Joe

1965
Aaron, Henry
Torre, Joe

Eddie Mathews (WHI IMAGE ID 54483)

MAGAZINES

Baseball Digest
Sport
The Sporting News
Sports Illustrated
Street & Smith Baseball Yearbooks

NEWSPAPERS

Eau Claire Leader-Telegram
Milwaukee Journal
Milwaukee Journal-Sentinel
Milwaukee Sentinel
Wisconsin State Journal

ORGANIZATIONS

Milwaukee Braves Historical Association
National Baseball Hall of Fame and Museum
Society for American Baseball Research

WEB SITES

www.atlantabraves.com
www.baseball-almanac.com
www.baseballhalloffame.org
www.baseballlibrary.com
www.baseball-reference.com
www.milwaukeebrewers.com
www.mlb.com
www.retrosheet.org
www.sportsencyclopedia.com

YEARBOOKS

1953–1965 Milwaukee Braves yearbooks
1966 Atlanta Braves yearbook

WORKS CITED

PROLOGUE

xi *I could visualize the old timers . . .*
Logan, Johnny. Interview with author, August 29, 2007.

xi *It's good to meet the people who were fans . . .*
Conley, Gene. Interview with author, August 30, 2007.

xii *Those fans were tremendous . . .*
Pafko, Andy. Interview with author, October 16, 2006.

xii *Anybody who played baseball in the 1950s and 1960s . . .*
Spahn, Warren. Guest of honor speech, Milwaukee Braves Historical Association Banquet, March 29, 2001.

xiii *Today, all I hear is, those old Braves were really great . . .*
Conley, Gene. Interview with author, August 30, 2007.

xiii *The idea of the association was to have banquets . . .*
Buege, Bob. Interview with author, August 29, 2007.

xiv *So when we talk about the Braves today and their place in history . . .*
Buege, Bob. Interview with author, August 29, 2007.

xiv *The banquet brought back memories of fifty years ago . . .*
Mantilla, Felix. Interview with author, August 30, 2007.

CHAPTER ONE

3 *Perini and the Braves were projected to lose approximately $1 million a year . . .*
Gendzel, Glen. "Competitive Boosterism: How Milwaukee Lost the Braves," *Business History Review,* Winter 1995, 530.

3 *He told us the Braves couldn't be competitive in Boston . . .*
Heller, Dick. "Milwaukee Went Batty as Home of Braves in '53," *Washington Times,* March 14, 2005, C14.

4 *We're moving to Milwaukee . . .*
Heller, Dick. "Milwaukee Went Batty as Home of Braves in '53," *Washington Times,* March 14, 2005, C14.

6 *You don't know all the letters, telegrams, and telephone calls . . .*
Kaese, Harold, and R.G. Lynch. *The Milwaukee Braves* (New York: Van Rees Press, 1954), 285.

8 *A Milwaukee baseball reporter named Sam Levy asked Perini if it was true . . .*
Mathews, Eddie, and Bob Buege. *Eddie Mathews and*

the National Pastime (Milwaukee: Douglas American Sports Publications, 1994), 78.

8 *The timing is bad right now . . .*
Bisher, Furman. *Miracle in Atlanta: The Atlanta Braves Story* (Cleveland, OH: The World Publishing Company, 1966), 22.

8 *There was no real opposition . . .*
Effrat, Louis. "The Braves New World," *New York Times, March 18, 1953. In The New York Times: Sports of the Times*, ed. William Taaffe and David Fischer (New York: St. Martin's Press, 2003), 92.

9 *Fine standing and prestige of Perini . . .*
Effrat, Louis. "The Braves New World." *New York Times, March 18, 1953. In The New York Times: Sports of the Times*, ed. William Taaffe and David Fischer (New York: St. Martin's Press, 2003), 92.

9 *I'll never forget, we're in spring training and we're playing the St. Louis Cardinals in St. Petersburg, Florida . . .*
Pafko, Andy. Interview with author, October 16, 2006.

9 *On the day the historic story broke . . .*
Grimm, Charlie, with Ed Prell. *Jolly Cholly's Story: Baseball, I Love You!* (Chicago: Henry Regnery Company, 1968), 195.

9 *Playing in the second-smallest city in the majors, population 725,000 . . .*
Schulian, John. "National Pastime: When It Was the Home of the Braves," *Sports Illustrated*, June 1, 1998, 106.

10 *If five years from now . . .*
Lynch, R.G. "The New Home of the New Braves," *Milwaukee Braves 1953 Yearbook,* (New York: Big League Books, 1953), 10.

10 *You can't imagine the complex situation which arose . . .*
Meany, Tom. *Milwaukee's Miracle Braves* (New York: Grosset & Dunlap, 1956), 10–11.

11 *People were bringing cash . . .*
Whiteside, Larry. "Last Stand in Boston," *The Boston Globe*, October 23, 1991, 63.

11 *You couldn't go into a store . . .*
Buege, Bob. Interview with author, August 29, 2007.

11 *Fans could join the Milwaukee Braves Booster Club . . .*
Kaese, Harold, and R.G. Lynch. *The Milwaukee Braves* (New York: Van Rees Press, 1954), 295.

12 *Despite the electric response . . .*
Grimm, Charlie, with Ed Prell. *Jolly Cholly's Story: Baseball, I Love You!* (Chicago: Henry Regnery Company, 1968), 196.

13 *This reception is getting better . . .*
Grimm, Charlie, with Ed Prell. *Jolly Cholly's Story: Baseball, I Love You!* (Chicago: Henry Regnery Company, 1968), 207.

13 *All along the route the people were packed three or four deep . . .*
Mathews, Eddie, and Bob Buege. *Eddie Mathews and the National Pastime* (Milwaukee: Douglas American Sports Publications, 1994), 82.

13 *The reaction of the players was something to see . . .*
Grimm, Charlie, with Ed Prell. *Jolly Cholly's Story: Baseball, I Love You!* (Chicago: Henry Regnery Company, 1968), 206.

13 *It would be hard to overstate . . .*
Mathews, Eddie, and Bob Buege. *Eddie Mathews and the National Pastime* (Milwaukee: Douglas American Sports Publications, 1994), 122.

13 *My ambition is to make Milwaukee . . .*
Gendzel, Glen. "Competitive Boosterism: How Milwaukee Lost the Braves," *Business History Review*, Winter 1995, 530.

13 *Allowing the Braves to pay just $1,000 a year to rent County Stadium . . .*
Lynch, R.G. "Report from Milwaukee: There's No Trouble in Paradise" *Sport*, May 1956, 80.

13 *More than anybody else . . .*
Mathews, Eddie, and Bob Buege. *Eddie Mathews and the National Pastime* (Milwaukee: Douglas American Sports Publications, 1994), 121.

15 *the greatest reception any ball club received from any town . . .*
Haudricourt, Tom. "A True Queen of Diamonds," *Milwaukee Journal Sentinel*, September 24, 2000, 02S.

15 *In Boston last year . . .*
Kaese, Harold, and R.G. Lynch. *The Milwaukee Braves* (New York: Van Rees Press, 1954), 300.

15 *I'll never forget the first game I pitched in Milwaukee . . .*
Spahn, Warren. "What the Series Feels Like" *Sport*, October 1959, 70.
Author's note: Warren Spahn, like all great pitchers, thought his first offering was a strike. Actually umpire Jocko Conlan thought it was low and called it a ball.

16 *Threw me a knuckleball . . .*
Heller, Dick. "Milwaukee Went Batty as Home of Braves in '53," *Washington Times*, March 14, 2005, C14.

16 *The ball slipped off his glove . . .*
Grimm, Charlie, with Ed Prell. *Jolly Cholly's Story: Baseball, I Love You!* (Chicago: Henry Regnery Company, 1968), 197.

17 *Keep this up . . .*
Grimm, Charlie, with Ed Prell. *Jolly Cholly's Story: Baseball, I Love You!* (Chicago: Henry Regnery Company, 1968), 197.

17 *Could run for mayor here tomorrow . . .*
Grimm, Charlie, with Ed Prell. *Jolly Cholly's Story: Baseball, I Love You!* (Chicago: Henry Regnery Company, 1968), 197.

17 *This is just the start . . .*
Grimm, Charlie, with Ed Prell. *Jolly Cholly's Story: Baseball, I Love You!* (Chicago: Henry Regnery Company, 1968), 197.

17 *A new ball club was born . . .*
Grimm, Charlie, with Ed Prell. *Jolly Cholly's Story: Baseball, I Love You!* (Chicago: Henry Regnery Company, 1968), 198.

18 *Joe's a good target out there . . .*
Silverman, Al. "They Don't Kid Adcock About His Hitting," *Sport*, August 1955, 83.

19 *I caught the ball with the good part of the bat . . .*
Meany, Tom. *Milwaukee's Miracle Braves* (New York: Grosset & Dunlap, 1956), 127.

19 *Gentlemen . . .*
Meany, Tom. *Milwaukee's Miracle Braves* (New York: Grosset & Dunlap, 1956), 128–129.

20 *Lou had a quality about him that you can't teach . . .*
Caruso, Gary. "Burdette Was No Joke," *ChopTalk*, March 2007, 57.

20 *He is big and strong . . .*
Meany, Tom. *Milwaukee's Miracle Braves* (New York: Grosset & Dunlap, 1956), 103.

20 *I back up first base and they yell . . .*
Meany, Tom. *Milwaukee's Miracle Braves* (New York: Grosset & Dunlap, 1956), 102.

20 *You've heard of the Gold Glove Award* . . .
Buege, Bob. "A Ballplayer's Ballplayer," *ChopTalk*, May 2007, 54.

20 *I'm proud to claim Johnny Logan as one of my boys* . . .
Grimm, Charlie, with Ed Prell. *Jolly Cholly's Story: Baseball, I Love You!* (Chicago: Henry Regnery Company, 1968), 209.

21 *He can make the play and he's strong and quick* . . .
Meany, Tom. *Milwaukee's Miracle Braves* (New York: Grosset & Dunlap, 1956), 160.

22 *In order to slow things down* . . .
Mathews, Eddie, and Bob Buege. *Eddie Mathews and the National Pastime* (Milwaukee: Douglas American Sports Publications, 1994), 86.

22 *It was the spitter* . . .
Grimm, Charlie, with Ed Prell. *Jolly Cholly's Story: Baseball, I Love You!* (Chicago: Henry Regnery Company, 1968), 205.

23 *The Braves thus became the first of the "area" Major League clubs* . . .
Grimm, Charlie, with Ed Prell. *Jolly Cholly's Story: Baseball, I Love You!* (Chicago: Henry Regnery Company, 1968), 200.

23 *Able to hold ten thousand cars comfortably* . . .
Hirschberg, Al. "Can Milwaukee Keep It Up?" *Sport*, February 1954, 81.

24 *The greatest thing that has happened to Milwaukee* . . .
Gendzel, Glen. "Competitive Boosterism: How Milwaukee Lost the Braves," *Business History Review*, Winter 1995, 530.

24 *Right from the beginning* . . .
Linn, Ed. "In Defense of the Milwaukee Fans," *Sport*, April 1958, 70.

25 *Boston has always meant home for me* . . .
Grimm, Charlie, with Ed Prell. *Jolly Cholly's Story: Baseball, I Love You!* (Chicago: Henry Regnery Company, 1968), 208.

25 *There are those enthusiastic youngsters you find in every baseball community* . . .
Pafko, Andy, as told to Dave Condon. "I'm Lucky to Be a Brave," *Sport*, June 1954, 26–27.

25 *Businesses gave us cases of Miller* . . .
Mishler, Todd. *Baseball in Beertown: America's Pastime in Milwaukee* (Black Earth, WI: Prairie Oak Press, 2005), 10.

25 *During those early days our dressing room was a madhouse* . . .
Grimm, Charlie, with Ed Prell. *Jolly Cholly's Story: Baseball, I Love You!* (Chicago: Henry Regnery Company, 1968), 201.

25 *The Braves individually profited by more than $100,000* . . .
Hirshberg, Al. "Can Milwaukee Keep It Up?" *Sport*, February 1954, 80.

26 *It surely was no coincidence* . . .
Caruso, Gary. *The Braves Encyclopedia* (Philadelphia: Temple University Press, 1995), 384.

26 *They had an Andy Pafko night* . . .
Pafko, Andy. Interview with author, October 16, 2006.

26 *I thought that I didn't have a chance* . . .
Pafko, Andy. Interview with author, October 16, 2006.

26 *During an era when a player's minimum salary was $7,500* . . .
Schulian, John. "National Pastime: When It Was the Home of the Braves," *Sports Illustrated*, June 1, 1998, 106.

51 *I was calm until the half inning was over . . .*
Hoffmann, Gregg. "Stan the Man the Star in '55," *Capital Times*, July 1, 2002, 1C.

51 *I was sitting in the dugout . . .*
Christl, Cliff. "Musial's Magic Capped 1955 Classic at County Stadium," *Milwaukee Journal Sentinel*, July 2, 2002, 01C.

51 *We gave a good account of ourselves . . .*
Christl, Cliff. "Musial's Magic Capped 1955 Classic at County Stadium," *Milwaukee Journal Sentinel*, July 2, 2002, 01C.

52 *We had a "tenth" player that year . . .*
Grimm, Charlie, with Ed Prell. *Jolly Cholly's Story: Baseball, I Love You!* (Chicago: Henry Regnery Company, 1968), 217.

53 *On a long-term basis . . .*
Lynch, R. G. "Report from Milwaukee: There's No Trouble in Paradise," *Sport*, May 1956: 36.

53 *The county collected approximately $471,000 in revenue . . .*
Lynch, R. G. . "Report from Milwaukee: There's No Trouble in Paradise," *Sport*, May 1956: 80.

54 *Aaron and Mathews had great years, but they couldn't carry the load . . .*
Grimm, Charlie, with Ed Prell. *Jolly Cholly's Story: Baseball, I Love You!* (Chicago: Henry Regnery Company, 1968), 217.

54 *I thought the notices were a bit premature . . .*
Grimm, Charlie, with Ed Prell. *Jolly Cholly's Story: Baseball, I Love You!* (Chicago: Henry Regnery Company, 1968), 217.

54 *He gave players a free rein . . .*
54, Donald, with Jesse Outlar. *Caught Short* (New York: Kingsport Press, Inc., 1972), 142.

54 *When the 1956 season opened, I was confident we would go all the way . . .*
Grimm, Charlie, with Ed Prell. *Jolly Cholly's Story: Baseball, I Love You!* (Chicago: Henry Regnery Company, 1968), 217.

55 *Certainly, Haney was there as a backup . . .*
Buege, Bob. Interview with author, August 29, 2007.

55 *Expectations were high for the Braves in 1956 . . .*
Mathews, Eddie, and Bob Buege. *Eddie Mathews and the National Pastime* (Milwaukee: Douglas American Sports Publications, 1994), 142.

55 *More than 900,000 tickets were sold before Opening Day . . .*
Lynch, R.G. "Report from Milwaukee: There's No Trouble in Paradise," *Sport*, May 1956, 80.

55 *Charlie Grimm will have the Milwaukee Braves in first place . . .*
Aaron, Henry, with Furman Bisher. *Aaron* (New York: Thomas Y. Crowell Company, 1974), 68.

56 *Before the game started against the Dodgers in Brooklyn . . .*
Grimm, Charlie, with Ed Prell. *Jolly Cholly's Story: Baseball, I Love You!* (Chicago: Henry Regnery Company, 1968), 218.

56 *I've decided to let someone else take a crack at the job . . .*
Klapisch, Bob, and Pete Van Wieren. *The Braves: An Illustrated History of America's Team* (Atlanta: Turner Publishing, Inc., 1995), 106.

57 *This is the toughest job I've ever faced . . .*
Lynch, Russ. "Which Way Milwaukee?" *Sport*, April 1957, 14.

57 *There is something magic about a change . . .*
Aaron, Henry, with Furman Bisher. *Aaron* (New York: Thomas Y. Crowell Company, 1974), 71.

57 *Sweeping the Dodgers that day gave us confidence . . .*
Mathews, Eddie, and Bob Buege. *Eddie Mathews and the National Pastime* (Milwaukee: Douglas American Sports Publications, 1994), 145.

58 *Believe me, I'm no miracle man . . .*
Buege, Bob. "Mini Manager," *ChopTalk*, June 2007, 54.

58 *I chipped some bones in my left elbow . . .*
Olderman, Murray. "Del Means Deliver," *Sports All Stars: Baseball* 1960, 23.

58 *Joe started down to first base rubbing his bifcep and mumbling to himself . . .*
Mathews, Eddie, and Bob Buege. *Eddie Mathews and the National Pastime* (Milwaukee: Douglas American Sports Publications, 1994), 141.

58 *When Joe charged the mound . . .*
Mathews, Eddie, and Bob Buege. *Eddie Mathews and the National Pastime* (Milwaukee: Douglas American Sports Publications, 1994), 141.

58 *Gomez went in there and got an ice pick . . .*
Schulian, John. "National Pastime: When It Was the Home of the Braves," *Sports Illustrated*, June 1, 1998, 106.

59 *He was a nasty pitcher and a fierce competitor . . .*
Aaron, Hank, with Lonnie Wheeler. *I Had a Hammer: The Hank Aaron Story* (New York: Harper Collins Publishers, 1991), 160.

59 *Until that happened . . .*
Wolf, Bob. "Buhl's in Control," *Sport*, October 1957, 37.

59 *When I joined the club . . .*
Wolf, Bob. "Buhl's in Control," *Sport*, October 1957, 37.

59 *Let's face it . . .*
Wolf, Bob. "Buhl's in Control," *Sport*, October 1957, 36.

61 *The more I pitched to a hitter . . .*
Bronsan, Jim. *Great Baseball Pitchers* (New York: Random House, 1965), 128.

61 *We had it. It was right there in our laps.*
Aaron, Henry, with Furman Bisher. *Aaron* (New York: Thomas Y. Crowell Company, 1974), 72.

61 *That was the key game . . .*
Aaron, Henry, with Furman Bisher. *Aaron* (New York: Thomas Y. Crowell Company, 1974), 73.

63 *Warren Spahn pitched his guts out in St. Louis . . .*
Aaron, Henry, with Furman Bisher. *Aaron* (New York: Thomas Y. Crowell Company, 1974), 73.

63 *All I was trying to do was get in front of it to block it . . .*
Mathews, Eddie, and Bob Buege. *Eddie Mathews and the National Pastime* (Milwaukee: Douglas American Sports Publications, 1994), 145.

63 *Beyond a doubt, that Saturday game in St. Louis . . .*
Aaron, Hank, with Lonnie Wheeler. *I Had a Hammer: The Hank Aaron Story* (New York: Harper Collins Publishers, 1991), 115.

63 *We might as well have left our bats in the clubhouse . . .*
Aaron, Henry, with Furman Bisher. *Aaron* (New York: Thomas Y. Crowell Company, 1974), 73.

63 *To this day, I believe . . .*
Aaron, Hank, with Lonnie Wheeler. *I Had a Hammer: The Hank Aaron Story* (New York: Harper Collins Publishers, 1991), 114.

63 *After the game, Quinn and I went to the top of the Chase Hotel for a drink . . .*
Davidson, Donald, with Jesse Outlar. *Caught Short* (New York: Kingsport Press, Inc., 1972), 57.

88 *It's just impossible to operate with parking facilities for only 700 cars . . .*
Reichler, Joe. "Baseball Has Got to Expand," *Sport*, April 1957, 91.

89 *There is demand for Major League Baseball around the country . . .*
Zimbalist, Andrew. *In the Best Interests of Baseball* (Hoboken, NJ: John Wiley & Sons, Inc., 2006), 67.

89 *I've got a face you can't forget . . .*
Spahn, Warren. "What the Series Feels Like," *Sport*, October 1959, 71.

89 *It appeared that John Quinn had built a dynasty.*
Davidson, Donald, with Jesse Outlar. *Caught Short* (New York: Kingsport Press, Inc., 1972), 56.

90 *All year the outfield was a matter of 'Who can play today?' . . .*
Mathews, Eddie, and Bob Buege. *Eddie Mathews and the National Pastime* (Milwaukee: Douglas American Sports Publications, 1994), 165.

90 *The other ballplayers were completely stunned and upset about it . . .*
Mathews, Eddie, and Bob Buege. *Eddie Mathews and the National Pastime* (Milwaukee: Douglas American Sports Publications, 1994), 166.

90 *I wasn't feeling that good . . .*
Hummel, Rick. "The Final Link," *ChopTalk*, February 2007, 54.

90 *It's a funny thing . . .*
Young, Dick. "Is Haney a Poor Manager?" *Sport*, July 1959, 91.

92 *Fred was Mr. Hollywood . . .*
Mathews, Eddie, and Bob Buege. *Eddie Mathews and the National Pastime* (Milwaukee: Douglas American Sports Publications, 1994), 144.

92 *I think in 1957 the country wanted us to win the pennant . . .*
Mathews, Eddie, and Bob Buege. *Eddie Mathews and the National Pastime* (Milwaukee: Douglas American Sports Publications, 1994), 175.

93 *The one thing that really held us up during the 1958 season . . .*
Aaron, Henry, with Furman Bisher. *Aaron* (New York: Thomas Y. Crowell Company, 1974), 113.

94 *They sure came through for me . . .*
Schaap, Dick. "Jay and Willey: Unlikely Roommates," *Sport*, April 1959, 40.

94 *We won the pennant by eight games that year . . .*
Aaron, Hank, with Lonnie Wheeler. *I Had a Hammer: The Hank Aaron Story* (New York: Harper Collins Publishers, 1991), 135.

94 *Declining attendance said the Braves' product . . .*
Mathews, Eddie, and Bob Buege. *Eddie Mathews and the National Pastime* (Milwaukee: Douglas American Sports Publications, 1994), 193.

94 *The Yankees didn't have much trouble getting to the World Series again, either . . .*
Aaron, Hank, with Lonnie Wheeler. *I Had a Hammer: The Hank Aaron Story* (New York: Harper Collins Publishers, 1991), 135.

94 *Whatever you do, don't get overconfident . . .*
Hirchberg, Al. *The Eddie Mathews Story* (New York: Julian Messner, Inc., 1960), 164.

96 *If you can win that first Series game, you're really floating along on clouds . . .*
Spahn, Warren. "What the Series Feels Like," *Sport*, October 1959, 72.

96 *Tension was thick in Game Two . . .*
Davidson, Donald, with Jesse Outlar. *Caught Short* (New York: Kingsport Press, Inc., 1972), 81.

96 *When we caught the plane to New York that night . . .*
Aaron, Henry, with Furman Bisher. *Aaron* (New York: Thomas Y. Crowell Company, 1974), 114.

98 *Now there was no question about it . . .*
Aaron, Henry, with Furman Bisher. *Aaron* (New York: Thomas Y. Crowell Company, 1974), 114.

98 *We found out the hard way that the Yankees . . .*
Spahn, Warren. "What the Series Feels Like," *Sport*, October 1959, 72.

98 *You could tell on the plane . . .*
Aaron, Henry, with Furman Bisher. *Aaron* (New York: Thomas Y. Crowell Company, 1974), 114.

100 *We thought we could beat them before the first game . . .*
Spahn, Warren. "What the Series Feels Like," *Sport*, October 1959, 72.

101 *I don't think I deserved the errors . . .*
Clines, Frank. "No Home Remedy Found for Game 7," *Milwaukee Journal Sentinel*, July 31, 1999, 6.

102 *The Yanks will play for one run at a time . . .*
Spahn, Warren. "What the Series Feels Like," *Sport*, October 1959, 72.

102 *There is a very narrow line between the team that wins the Series . . .*
Spahn, Warren. "What the Series Feels Like," *Sport*, October 1959, 70.

103 *We didn't think we could lose two straight in Milwaukee . . .*
Aaron, Hank, with Lonnie Wheeler. *I Had a Hammer: The Hank Aaron Story* (New York: Harper Collins Publishers, 1991), 135.

103 *The turning point was in our bats . . .*
Clines, Frank. "No Home Remedy Found for Game 7," *Milwaukee Journal Sentinel*, July 31, 1999, 6.

103 *It was the beginning of the end . . .*
Davidson, Donald, with Jesse Outlar. *Caught Short* (New York: Kingsport Press, Inc., 1972), 80.

CHAPTER FOUR

105 *During Tebbetts' managing tour with Cincinnati . . .*
Caruso, Gary. *The Braves Encyclopedia* (Philadelphia: Temple University Press, 1995), 305.

105 *Quinn had been a loyal employee . . .*
Mathews, Eddie, and Bob Buege. *Eddie Mathews and the National Pastime* (Milwaukee: Douglas American Sports Publications, 1994), 211.

105 *I never could figure why John Quinn got bounced out of his job . . .*
Aaron, Henry, with Furman Bisher. *Aaron* (New York: Thomas Y. Crowell Company, 1974), 118.

106 *Many people thought Perini made a big mistake . . .*
Mathews, Eddie, and Bob Buege. *Eddie Mathews and the National Pastime* (Milwaukee: Douglas American Sports Publications, 1994), 203.

106 *You can imagine, I guess, what spring training was like . . .*
Aaron, Henry, with Furman Bisher. *Aaron* (New York: Thomas Y. Crowell Company, 1974), 118.

106 *We were just going through the motions . . .*
Aaron, Henry, with Furman Bisher. *Aaron* (New York: Thomas Y. Crowell Company, 1974), 117.

106 *Leadership is hard to define . . .*
Mathews, Eddie, and Bob Buege. *Eddie Mathews and the National Pastime* (Milwaukee: Douglas American Sports Publications, 1994), 183.

108 *Henry is capable of hitting .400 . . .*
Gutman, Bill. *Henry Aaron* (New York: Tempo Books, 1974), 40.

108 *I think the umpires liked me, because I made their job easy . . .*
Aaron, Hank, with Lonnie Wheeler. *I Had a Hammer: The Hank Aaron Story* (New York: Harper Collins Publishers, 1991), 105.

108 *I wasn't hit that much. . . . But I got thrown at quite a bit . . .*
Lea, Bud. "Aaron Will Always Be a Hero Here," *The Tepee Newsletter*, September 2004, 1.

108 *It's that loping gait of his . . .*
Kahn, Roger. *Beyond the Boys of Summer* (New York: McGraw-Hill, 2005), 105.

108 *He was never a flashy player . . .*
Hummel, Rick. "The Final Link," *ChopTalk*, February 2007, 55.

109 *I'll never forget that play . . .*
Anderson, Dave. "Baseball's Perfect 12," *New York Times*, May 18, 1981, Section C, 4.

110 *He hadn't seen the ball clear the fence . . .*
Mathews, Eddie, and Bob Buege. *Eddie Mathews and the National Pastime*, (Milwaukee: Douglas American Sports Publications, 1994), 182.

110 *That was the real story . . .*
Mathews, Eddie, and Bob Buege. *Eddie Mathews and the National Pastime* (Milwaukee: Douglas American Sports Publications, 1994), 183.

111 *Who pitched the greatest ballgame ever . . .*
Buege, Bob. "Thanks for the Memories, Lew," *The Tepee Newsletter*, April 2007, 3.

111 *Haney had been hired to replace the easy-going Charlie Grimm . . .*
Buege, Bob. *The Milwaukee Braves: A Baseball Eulogy* (Milwaukee: Douglas American Sports Publications, 1988), 225.

111 *Fred Haney had a different way of managing . . .*
Mathews, Eddie, and Bob Buege. *Eddie Mathews and the National Pastime* (Milwaukee: Douglas American Sports Publications, 1994), 187.

111 *Ballplayers are the poorest possible judges of a manager's ability . . .*
Young, Dick. "Is Haney a Poor Manager?" *Sport*, July 1959, 16.

113 *I thought a lot of players were unconsciously sitting back . . .*
Furlong, Bill. "Milwaukee's Trouble: Too Many Stars Are Hard to Handle," *Sport*, March 1960, 72.

113 *I don't know what we would have done without him . . .*
Olderman, Murray. "Del Means Deliver," *Sports All Stars: Baseball*, 1960, 22.

113 *He hardly played any at all . . .*
Aaron, Henry, with Furman Bisher. *Aaron* (New York: Thomas Y. Crowell Company, 1974), 119.

114 *The situation had certain similarities to 1956 . . .*
Mathews, Eddie, and Bob Buege. *Eddie Mathews and the National Pastime* (Milwaukee: Douglas American Sports Publications, 1994), 186.

114 *As far as we were concerned . . .*
Aaron, Hank, with Lonnie Wheeler. *I Had a Hammer: The Hank Aaron Story* (New York: Harper Collins Publishers, 1991), 141.

114 *After playing in front of big crowds for so many years . . .*
Mathews, Eddie, and Bob Buege. *Eddie Mathews and the National Pastime* (Milwaukee: Douglas American Sports Publications, 1994), 186.

115 *On the plane to Los Angeles that night . . .*
Aaron, Henry, with Furman Bisher. *Aaron* (New York: Thomas Y. Crowell Company, 1974), 121.

115 *We looked truly superior . . .*
Aaron, Henry, with Furman Bisher. *Aaron* (New York: Thomas Y. Crowell Company, 1974), 122.

115 *You still had to like our chances with McMahon going . . .*
Aaron, Henry, with Furman Bisher. *Aaron* (New York: Thomas Y. Crowell Company, 1974), 122.

116 *The sight of Spahn, our ace, warming up in the bullpen . . .*
Aaron, Henry, with Furman Bisher. *Aaron* (New York: Thomas Y. Crowell Company, 1974), 122.

116 *Nobody blamed Felix . . .*
Mathews, Eddie, and Bob Buege. *Eddie Mathews and the National Pastime* (Milwaukee: Douglas American Sports Publications, 1994), 187.

117 *I've never heard such loud water in my life . . .*
Aaron, Henry, with Furman Bisher. *Aaron* (New York: Thomas Y. Crowell Company, 1974), 124.

117 *Maybe the novelty had worn off . . .*
Mathews, Eddie, and Bob Buege. *Eddie Mathews and the National Pastime* (Milwaukee: Douglas American Sports Publications, 1994), 191.

117 *The 1959 season had been filled with so much promise . . .*
Caruso, Gary. *The Braves Encyclopedia* (Philadelphia: Temple University Press, 1995), 87.

117 *I think Haney is the most underrated manager I've known . . .*
Davidson, Donald, with Jesse Outlar. *Caught Short* (New York: Kingsport Press, Inc., 1972), 62.

117 *We had better take stock of ourselves . . .*
Furlong, Bill. "Milwaukee's Trouble: Too Many Stars Are Hard to Handle," *Sport*, March 1960, 15.

117 *Remember, Haney didn't build this club; it was here when he came . . .*
Furlong, Bill. "Milwaukee's Trouble: Too Many Stars Are Hard to Handle," *Sport*, March 1960, 15.

117 *When they announced Haney was out, you can bet few players were sorry . . .*
Furlong, Bill. "Milwaukee's Trouble: Too Many Stars Are Hard to Handle," *Sport*, March 1960, 14.

118 *I still had no feeling at the time . . .*
Aaron, Henry, with Furman Bisher. *Aaron* (New York: Thomas Y. Crowell Company, 1974), 115, 126.

119 *[Charlie Dressen] . . . took over a very talented and very difficult club . . .*
Bragan, Bobby, as told to Jeff Guinn. *You Can't Hit the Ball with the Bat on Your Shoulder* (Fort Worth, TX: The Summit Group, 1992), 291.

119 *He never managed a ball game . . .*
Caruso, Gary. *The Braves Encyclopedia* (Philadelphia: Temple University Press, 1995), 305.

119 *Wherever he was, Dressen was always controversial . . .*
Mathews, Eddie, and Bob Buege. *Eddie Mathews and the National Pastime* (Milwaukee: Douglas American Sports Publications, 1994), 194.

119 *I honestly don't know, but write this down . . .*
Rosenthal, Harold. *Baseball's Best Managers* (New York: Bartholomew House, Inc., 1961), 72.

119 *Dressen knew as much about baseball as any manager in the game . . .*
Aaron, Hank, with Lonnie Wheeler. *I Had a Hammer: The Hank Aaron Story* (New York: Harper Collins Publishers, 1991), 155.

120 *Another thing that hurt us was that we had 12 games rained out the first part of the season . . .*
Graham Jr., Frank. "The Inside Story of the Braves Dissension," *Sport*, February 1962, 86.

120 *The biggest disappointment on the Braves' 1960 staff was Don McMahon . . .*
Graham Jr., Frank. "The Inside Story of the Braves Dissension," *Sport*, February 1962, 86.

121 *I had him out by a mile . . .*
Mathews, Eddie, and Bob Buege. *Eddie Mathews and the National Pastime* (Milwaukee: Douglas American Sports Publications, 1994), 198.

121 *"Frank, don't come in here like that . . ."*
Mathews, Eddie, and Bob Buege. *Eddie Mathews and the National Pastime* (Milwaukee: Douglas American Sports Publications, 1994), 199.

121 *Charlie believed in club discipline . . .*
Davidson, Donald, with Jesse Outlar. *Caught Short* (New York: Kingsport Press, Inc., 1972), 140.

122 *Spahn and Burdette used to make Dressen's life miserable . . .*
Torre, Joe, with Tom Verducci. *Chasing the Dream: My Lifelong Journey to the World Series* (New York: Bantam Books, 1997), 95.

122–123 *The hot foot was just epidemic in baseball . . .*
Uecker, Bob, and Mickey Herskowitz. *Catcher in the Wry* (New York: Jove Books, 1982), 139.

123 *He had good control, moved the ball around and threw that sinker . . .*
Caruso, Gary. "Passing of a Legend," *ChopTalk*, March 2007, 33.

125 *If he hadn't pitched his no-hitter, I don't think I would have gotten mine . . .*
Reichler, Joseph. *30 Years of Baseball's Great Moments* (New York: Crown Publishers, Inc., 1974), 94.

125 *We were all getting older . . .*
Mathews, Eddie, and Bob Buege. *Eddie Mathews and the National Pastime* (Milwaukee: Douglas American Sports Publications, 1994), 203.

125 *What really hurt was losing the young Braves . . .*
Aaron, Hank, with Lonnie Wheeler. *I Had a Hammer: The Hank Aaron Story* (New York: Harper Collins Publishers, 1991), 157.

126 *He wasn't much with the stick . . .*
Mathews, Eddie, and Bob Buege. *Eddie Mathews and the National Pastime* (Milwaukee: Douglas American Sports Publications, 1994), 206.

126 *That move made no sense to us . . .*
Mathews, Eddie, and Bob Buege. *Eddie Mathews and the National Pastime* (Milwaukee: Douglas American Sports Publications, 1994), 204.

126 *Johnny was great for team spirit . . .*
Aaron, Henry, with Furman Bisher. *Aaron* (New York: Thomas Y. Crowell Company, 1974), 130.

126 *He hit quite a few home runs for us and gave us help in the outfield . . .*
Mathews, Eddie, and Bob Buege. *Eddie Mathews and the National Pastime* (Milwaukee: Douglas American Sports Publications, 1994), 207.

126 *The Braves' personality was being changed . . .*
Aaron, Henry, with Furman Bisher. *Aaron* (New York: Thomas Y. Crowell Company, 1974), 132.

126 *That happened to be the first spring camp . . .*
Torre, Joe, with Tom Verducci. *Chasing the Dream: My Lifelong Journey to the World Series* (New York: Bantam Books, 1997), 86.

127 *I wish I could say that we were a better team . . .*
Aaron, Hank, with Lonnie Wheeler. *I Had a Hammer: The Hank Aaron Story* (New York: Harper Collins Publishers, 1991), 155.

127 *The people on the county board, which controlled the stadium, got greedy . . .*
Mathews, Eddie, and Bob Buege. *Eddie Mathews and the National Pastime* (Milwaukee: Douglas American Sports Publications, 1994), 191.

127 *I knew my arm and I knew my hitters . . .*
Kahn, Roger. *The Head Game: Baseball Seen from the Pitcher's Mound* (New York: Harcourt, Inc., 2000), 175.

128 *It was so easy, it was pathetic . . .*
Reichler, Joseph. *30 Years of Baseball's Great Moments* (New York: Crown Publishers, Inc., 1974), 94.

128 *Here I waited nearly a lifetime to get my no-hitter . . .*
Reichler, Joseph. *30 Years of Baseball's Great Moments* (New York: Crown Publishers, Inc., 1974), 94.

128 *You're satisfied if you get two in a game . . .*
Reichler, Joseph. *30 Years of Baseball's Great Moments* (New York: Crown Publishers, Inc., 1974), 105.

128 *Losing Del hurt us . . .*
Mathews, Eddie, and Bob Buege. *Eddie Mathews and the National Pastime* (Milwaukee: Douglas American Sports Publications, 1994), 207.

128 *[Del Crandall's] backup, Charlie Lau, who became a famous hitting coach . . .*
Torre, Joe, with Tom Verducci. *Chasing the Dream: My Lifelong Journey to the World Series* (New York: Bantam Books, 1997), 89.

128 *Spahn and Burdette were like older brothers . . .*
Torre, Joe, with Tom Verducci. *Chasing the Dream: My Lifelong Journey to the World Series* (New York: Bantam Books, 1997), 95.

129 *Mathews and I used to sit in the clubhouse playing a card game called casino . . .*
Aaron, Hank, with Lonnie Wheeler. *I Had a Hammer: The Hank Aaron Story* (New York: Harper Collins Publishers, 1991), 156.

131 *I have always thought that one remark typified him . . .*
Uecker, Bob, and Mickey Herskowitz. *Catcher in the Wry* (New York: Jove Books, 1982), 205.

131 *Before I got close, I wasn't too excited about it . . .*
Klapisch, Bob, and Pete Van Wieren. *The Braves: An Illustrated History of America's Team* (Atlanta: Turner Publishing, Inc., 1995), 132.

131–132 *That was my biggest personal thrill . . .*
Bronsan, Jim. *Great Baseball Pitchers* (New York: Random House, 1965), 137.

132 *The general impression was that Dressen had lost control of the players . . .*
Aaron, Henry, with Furman Bisher. *Aaron* (New York: Thomas Y. Crowell Company, 1974), 145.

133 *We finished the ballgame, walked into the clubhouse . . .*
Mathews, Eddie, and Bob Buege. *Eddie Mathews and the National Pastime* (Milwaukee: Douglas American Sports Publications, 1994), 210.

133 *Dressen did a good job . . .*
Graham Jr., Frank. "The Inside Story of the Braves Dissension," *Sport*, February 1962, 37.

133 *I wasn't really happy there . . .*
Graham Jr., Frank. "The Inside Story of the Braves Dissension," *Sport*, February 1962, 37.

133 *Tebbetts seemed like an odd choice for the Braves . . .*
Mathews, Eddie, and Bob Buege. *Eddie Mathews and the National Pastime* (Milwaukee: Douglas American Sports Publications, 1994), 211.

133 *Nineteen sixty-one was the first year in a long time . . .*
Mathews, Eddie, and Bob Buege. *Eddie Mathews and the National Pastime* (Milwaukee: Douglas American Sports Publications, 1994), 210.

CHAPTER FIVE

136 *One of the planks in Allen's platform . . .*
Bisher, Furman. *Miracle in Atlanta: The Atlanta Braves Story* (Cleveland, OH: The World Publishing Company, 1966), 8, 10.

136 *When Tebbetts joined the Braves as a vice-president . . .*
Davidson, Donald, with Jesse Outlar. *Caught Short* (New York: Kingsport Press, Inc., 1972), 145.

137 *There's no telling what he'd have done . . .*
Caruso, Gary. *The Braves Encyclopedia* (Philadelphia: Temple University Press, 1995), 91.

137 *I would be hailed as the first Milwaukee native to play for the Braves . . .*
Uecker, Bob, and Mickey Herskowitz. *Catcher in the Wry* (New York: Jove Books, 1982), 26.

138 *The Braves had declined from their World Series years, '57 and '58 . . .*
Uecker, Bob, and Mickey Herskowitz. *Catcher in the Wry* (New York: Jove Books, 1982), 28.

138 *Every night at County Stadium . . .*
Torre, Joe, with Tom Verducci. *Chasing the Dream: My Lifelong Journey to the World Series* (New York: Bantam Books, 1997), 106.

138 *I became a cold-weather catcher . . .*
Torre, Joe, with Tom Verducci. *Chasing the Dream: My Lifelong Journey to the World Series* (New York: Bantam Books, 1997), 99.

139 *Perini at that time hardly ever came to Milwaukee to see the ballclub . . .*
Mathews, Eddie, and Bob Buege. *Eddie Mathews and the National Pastime* (Milwaukee: Douglas American Sports Publications, 1994), 221.

139 *Perini placed 1,500,000 shares of stock on the open market . . .*
Katz, Fred. "Lou Perini: Absentee Owner," *Sport*, May 1962, 47.

139 *The ballplayers never paid much attention to any of that stuff . . .*
Mathews, Eddie, and Bob Buege. *Eddie Mathews and the National Pastime* (Milwaukee: Douglas American Sports Publications, 1994), 221.

139 *His snapping fastball was gone . . .*
Uecker, Bob, and Mickey Herskowitz. *Catcher in the Wry* (New York: Jove Books, 1982), 204.

140 *Sometimes I get behind on batters deliberately . . .*
Bronsan, Jim. *Great Baseball Pitchers* (New York: Random House, 1965), 135.

140 *I never went in the trainer's room . . .*
Semrau, Dennis. "Spahn, Crandall Recall Grand Era," *Capital Times*, September 28, 2000, 5C.

140 *Instead of a transfusion of young blood and fresh talent . . .*
Mathews, Eddie, and Bob Buege. *Eddie Mathews and the National Pastime* (Milwaukee: Douglas American Sports Publications, 1994), 230.

141 *When the umpire ruled in the Braves' favor . . .*
Caruso, Gary. *The Braves Encyclopedia* (Philadelphia: Temple University Press, 1995), 306.

141 *Although he had reaped $7.5 million in profits . . .*
Gendzel, Glen. "Competitive Boosterism: How Milwaukee Lost the Braves," *Business History Review*, Winter 1995, 530.

142 *Young sportsmen who are more interested . . .*
Gendzel, Glen. "Competitive Boosterism: How Milwaukee Lost the Braves," *Business History Review,* Winter 1995, 530.

142 *The whole deal had the uncomfortable smell . . .*
Veeck, Bill, with Ed Linn. "Another Gone with the Wind," *Sports Illustrated,* June 7, 1965, 34.

142 *Purchasing all but 10 percent of the Braves for $6,218,480 . . .*
Gendzel, Glen. "Competitive Boosterism: How Milwaukee Lost the Braves," *Business History Review,* Winter 1995, 530.

142 *Bartholomay and his associates offered to sell 115,000 shares of team stock at a price of $10 per share . . .*
Bisher, Furman. *Miracle in Atlanta: The Atlanta Braves Story* (Cleveland, OH: The World Publishing Company, 1966), 25.

142 *If there had been a market for it, the club would probably still be in Milwaukee . . .*
Davidson, Donald, with Jesse Outlar. *Caught Short* (New York: Kingsport Press, Inc., 1972), 90.

143 *We never considered the possibility of the Braves leaving town . . .*
Aaron, Hank, with Lonnie Wheeler. *I Had a Hammer: The Hank Aaron Story* (New York: Harper Collins Publishers, 1991), 163.

143 *A Braves fan returning to County Stadium . . .*
Buege, Bob. *The Milwaukee Braves: A Baseball Eulogy* (Milwaukee: Douglas American Sports Publications, 1988), 342.

143–144 *Mr. Perini was in the process of building up an entire side of the city . . .*
Aaron, Hank, with Lonnie Wheeler. *I Had a Hammer: The Hank Aaron Story* (New York: Harper Collins Publishers, 1991), 169.

144 *From the first day Bobby arrived . . .*
Bragan, Bobby, as told to Jeff Guinn. *You Can't Hit the Ball with the Bat on Your Shoulder* (Fort Worth, TX: The Summit Group, 1992), 291.

144 *He could really get on your case . . .*
Uecker, Bob, and Mickey Herskowitz. *Catcher in the Wry* (New York: Jove Books, 1982), 140.

144 *We had the feeling Bobby Bragan was there as a hatchet man . . .*
Bragan, Bobby, as told to Jeff Guinn. *You Can't Hit the Ball with the Bat on Your Shoulder* (Fort Worth, TX: The Summit Group, 1992), 291, 311.

144 *When the '63 season began, Del Crandall was still first-string catcher . . .*
Bragan, Bobby, as told to Jeff Guinn. *You Can't Hit the Ball with the Bat on Your Shoulder* (Fort Worth, TX: The Summit Group, 1992), 285.

144 *Bobby probably knew as much baseball as any of the Braves managers . . .*
Davidson, Donald, with Jesse Outlar. *Caught Short* (New York: Kingsport Press, Inc., 1972), 146.

144 *I'm sure I would have been a better manager . . .*
Bragan, Bobby, as told to Jeff Guinn. *You Can't Hit the Ball with the Bat on Your Shoulder* (Fort Worth, TX: The Summit Group, 1992), 279.

144 *I'd like to think I let Lou pitch the first game . . .*
Bragan, Bobby, as told to Jeff Guinn. *You Can't Hit the Ball with the Bat on Your Shoulder* (Fort Worth, TX: The Summit Group, 1992), 278, 279.

145 *Despite the fact that the team was falling apart around him . . .*
Aaron, Hank, with Lonnie Wheeler. *I Had a Hammer: The Hank Aaron Story* (New York: Harper Collins Publishers, 1991), 165.

167 *We were a club that could pound the ball as well as anyone* . . .
Torre, Joe, with Tom Verducci. *Chasing the Dream: My Lifelong Journey to the World Series* (New York: Bantam Books, 1997), 102.

168 *We were never terrible but almost always barely a notch* . . .
Torre, Joe, with Tom Verducci. *Chasing the Dream: My Lifelong Journey to the World Series* (New York: Bantam Books, 1997), 101.

168 *The team lost nearly $1 million while playing out a season that no one wanted* . . .
Gendzel, Glen. "Competitive Boosterism: How Milwaukee Lost the Braves," *Business History Review*, Winter 1995, 530.

169 *Gave baseball an irresponsible, gypsy look.*
Gendzel, Glen. "Competitive Boosterism: How Milwaukee Lost the Braves," *Business History Review*, Winter 1995, 530.

169 *Milwaukee is an excellent baseball town* . . .
Zimbalist, Andrew. *In the Best Interests of Baseball* (Hoboken, NJ: John Wiley & Sons, Inc., 2006), 118.

169 *There were so many appeals and rulings, restraining orders and injunctions* . . .
Bisher, Furman. *Miracle in Atlanta: The Atlanta Braves Story* (Cleveland, OH: The World Publishing Company, 1966), 176.

171 *There is as much chance of the Braves playing in Milwaukee this summer* . . .
Klapisch, Bob, and Pete Van Wieren. *The Braves: An Illustrated History of America's Team* (Atlanta: Turner Publishing, Inc., 1995), 135.

171 *The 12,577 mourners who attended the graveside ceremony* . . .
Buege, Bob. *The Milwaukee Braves: A Baseball Eulogy* (Milwaukee: Douglas American Sports Publications, 1988), 407.

172 *As you might expect, that was a very emotional night* . . .
Mathews, Eddie, and Bob Buege. *Eddie Mathews and the National Pastime* (Milwaukee: Douglas American Sports Publications, 1994), 253.

172 *When the game ended* . . .
Mathews, Eddie, and Bob Buege. *Eddie Mathews and the National Pastime* (Milwaukee: Douglas American Sports Publications, 1994), 253.

INDEX

ABOUT THE AUTHOR

Native Wisconsinite and University of Wisconsin–Oshkosh graduate William Povletich has a wide array of experience in the film and television industry and as a writer. His projects have earned both critical acclaim and audience success. In 2005 Povletich was a supervising producer on the History Channel documentary *Rwanda: Do Scars Ever Fade?* which earned a 2005 Peabody Award and an Emmy nomination for Outstanding Informational Program. As associate producer on the History Channel's *Inside Pol Pot's Secret Prison*, he was nominated for two National News and Documentary Emmy Awards in 2003; *Inside Pol Pot's Secret Prison* was named Best Documentary in a Continuing Series for the prestigious 2002 International Documentary Association Distinguished Achievement Awards.

Povletich's documentary film *Henry Aaron's Summer Up North* chronicled the living legend's struggles and successes in one important, if not trying, summer of minor-league baseball in the northwoods community of Eau Claire, Wisconsin. The film was an official selection to the 2006 National Baseball Hall of Fame Film Festival and the 2005 Wisconsin Film Festival. Povletich was also an executive producer on the one-hour television special *Milwaukee Braves: The Golden Legacy* for Fox Sports Net, the exclusive fiftieth-anniversary tribute to the 1957 World Series champions. His PBS documentary *A Braves New World*, produced through Milwaukee Public Television, further explores the Braves' legacy in Milwaukee.

Povletich is the author of *Green Bay Packers: Legends in Green and Gold* and "When the Braves of Bushville Ruled Baseball: Celebrating Andy Pafko and the 1957 Milwaukee Braves" for the *Wisconsin Magazine of History*.